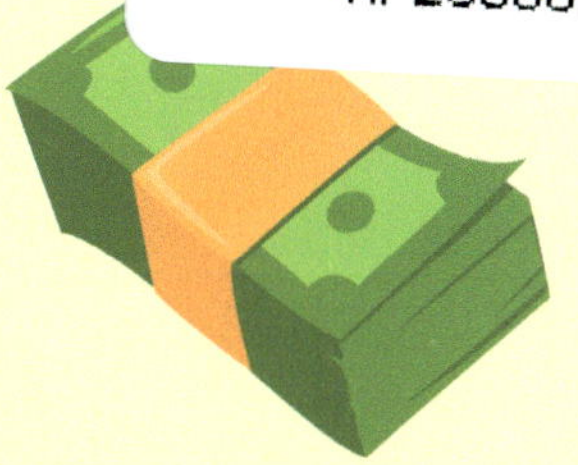

Vision Board Manifestation Book For Black Women

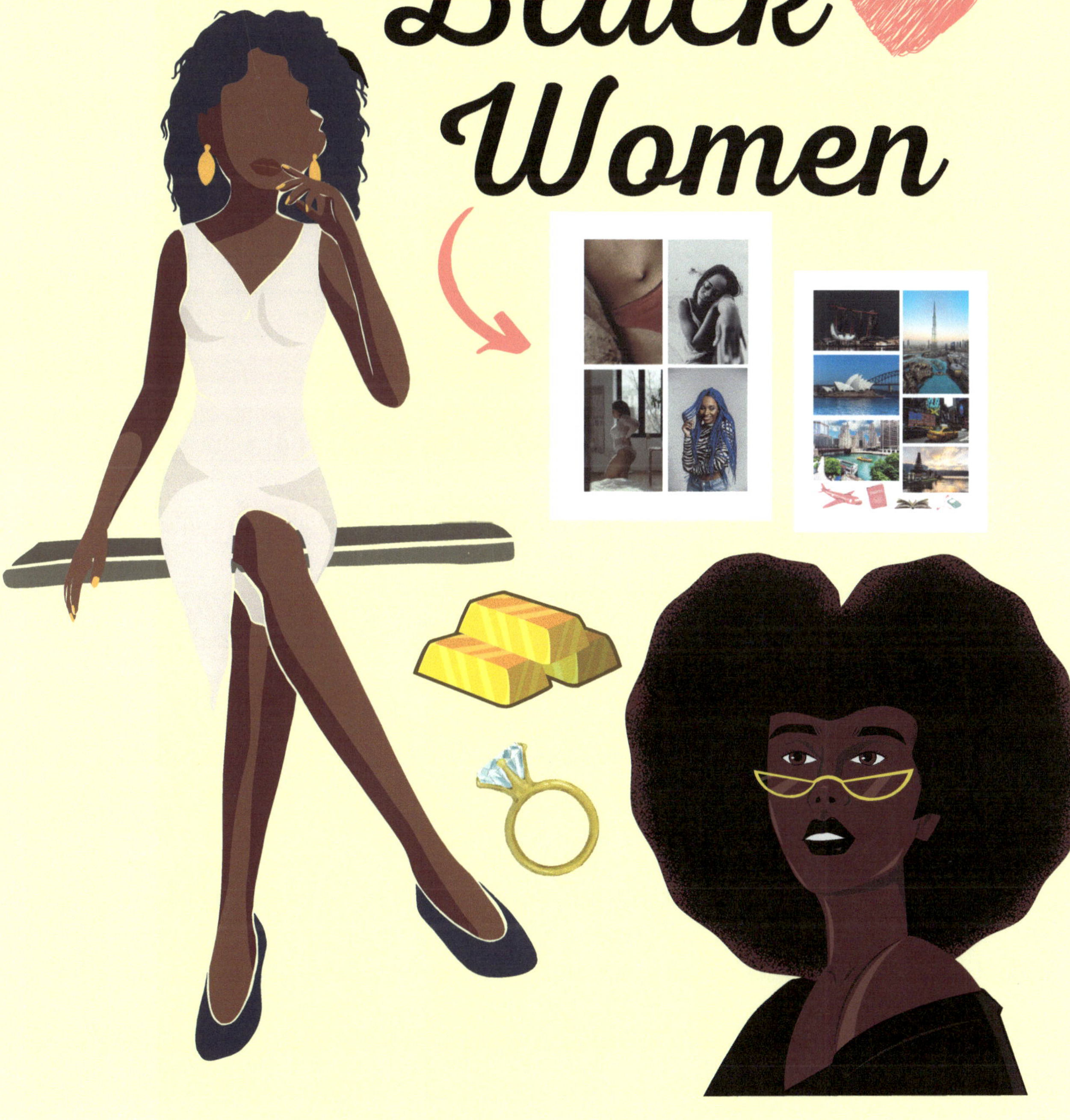

Journee Williams © 2022

Chapters:

1: Love & Relationships

2: Family

3: Wealth

4: Business & Career

5: Spirituality, God & The Universe

6: Property, Land, New House

7: New Cars

8: Beauty & Fashion

9: Fun, Hobbies & Sports

10: Body Positivity & Health

11: Vacations

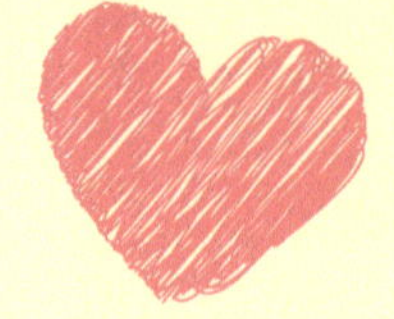

How to use: Use each as you please, and take what you need to manifest in your own life! If any of the images don't resonate with you, you don't need to cut them out to add them to your vision board!

1: Love & Relationships

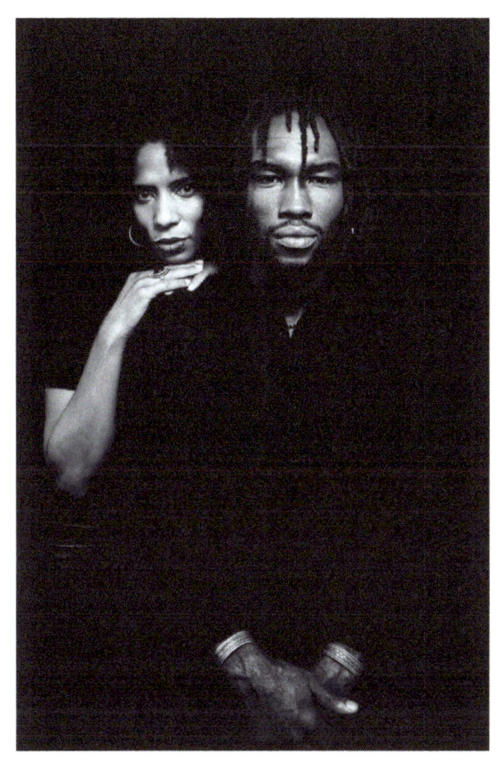

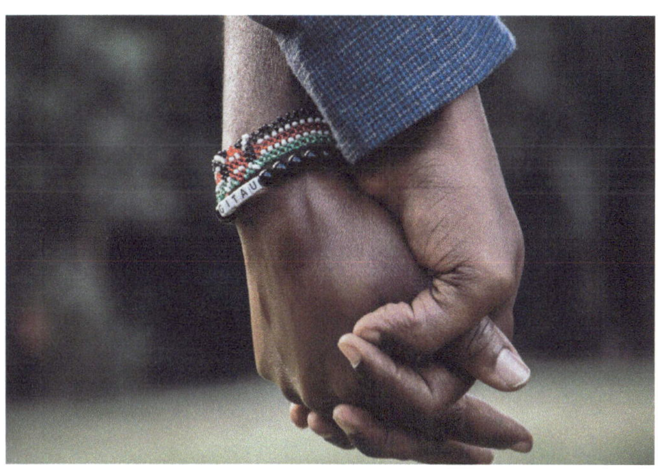

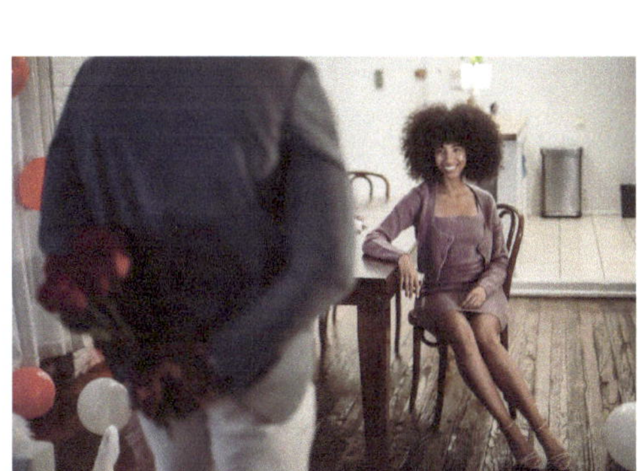

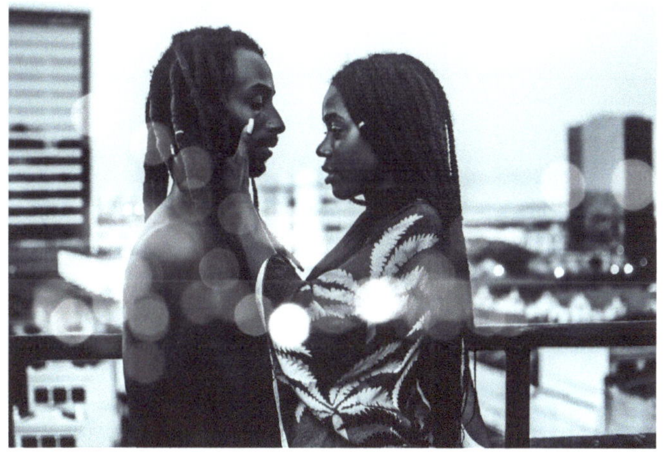

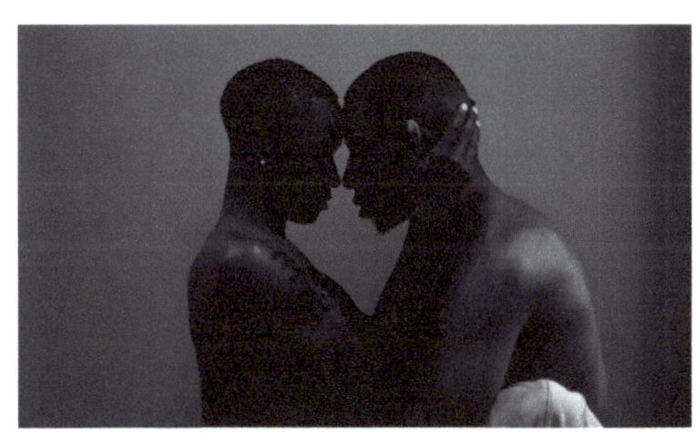

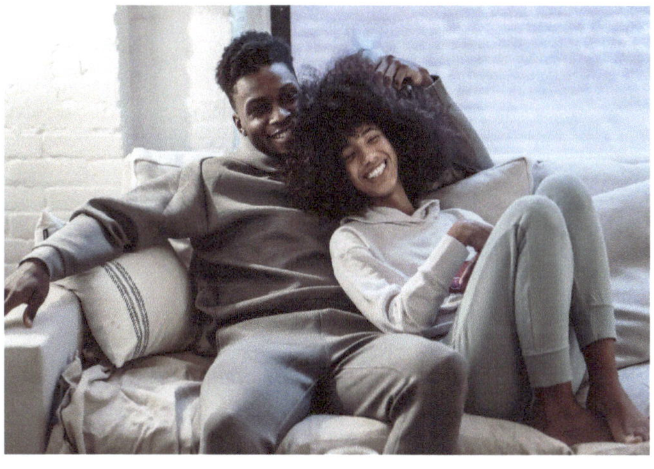

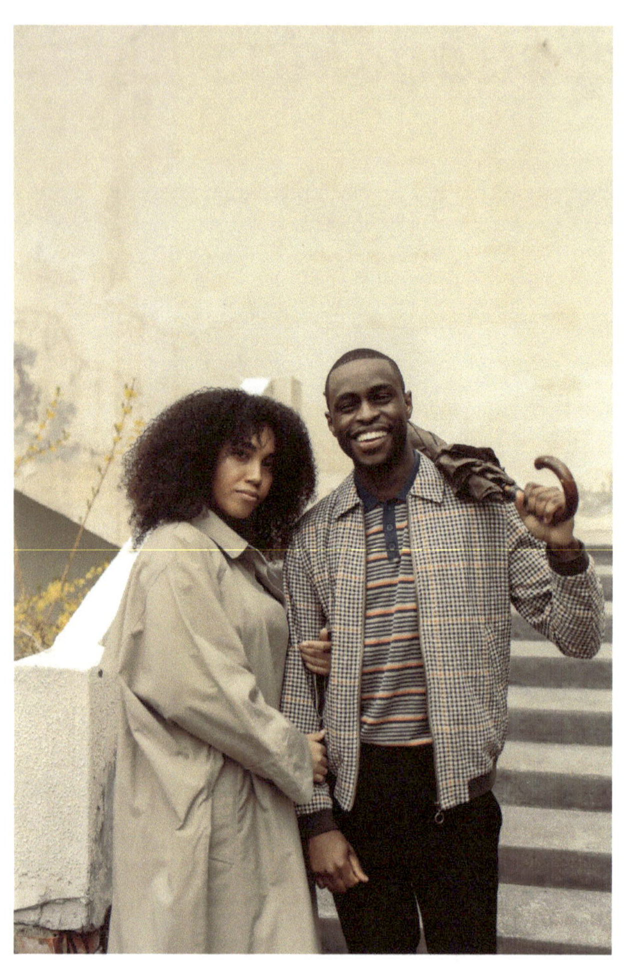
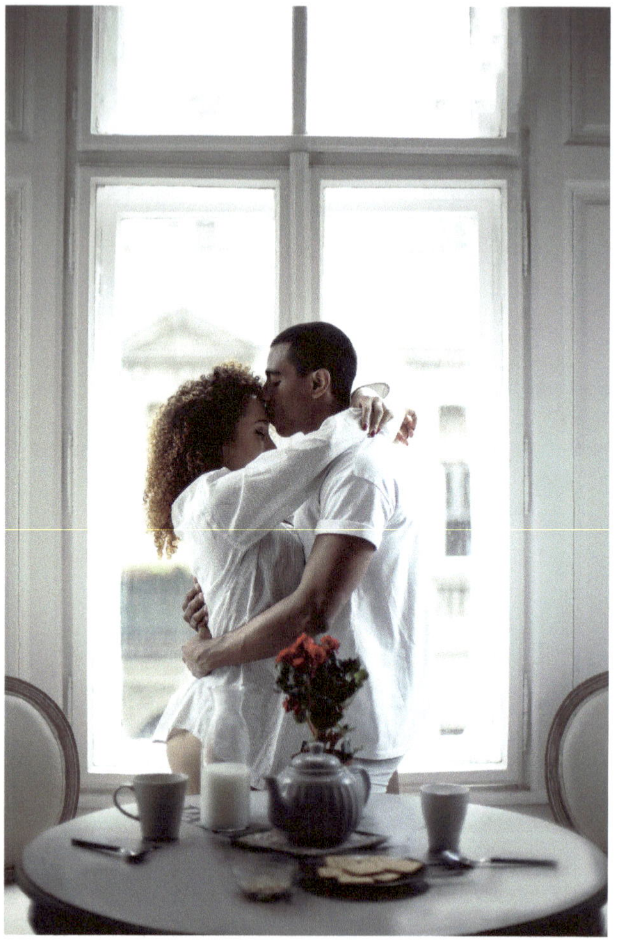
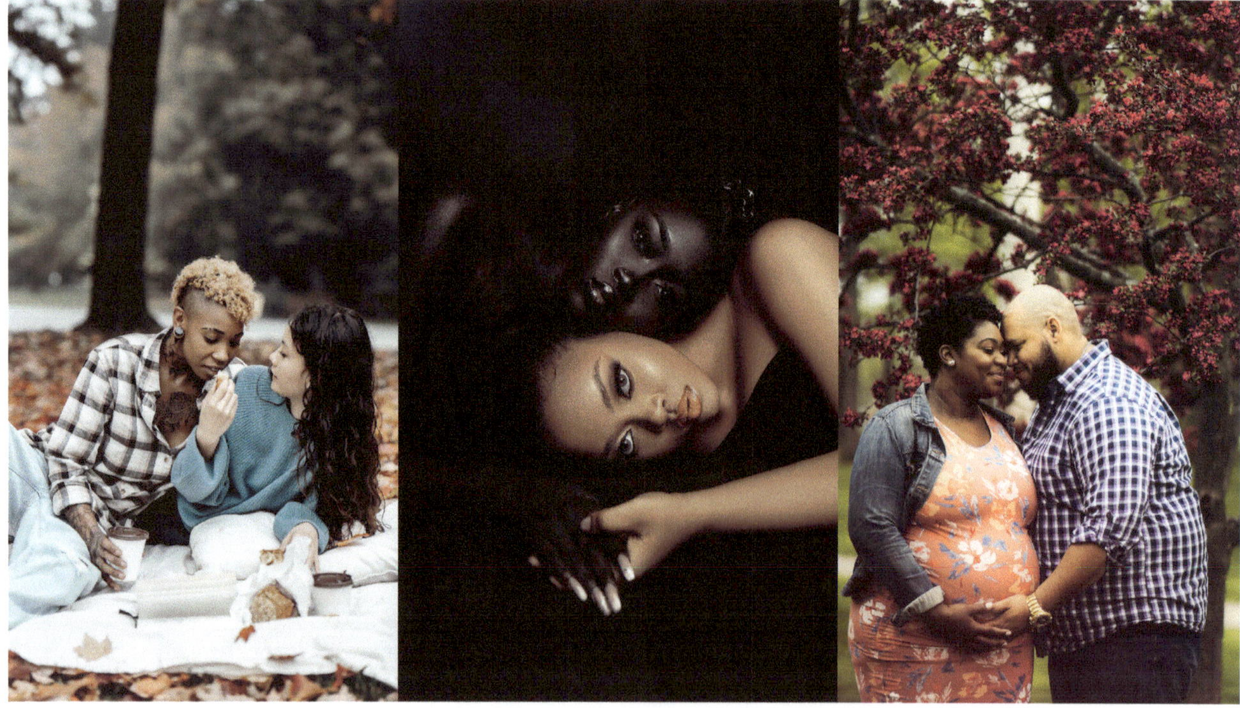

love

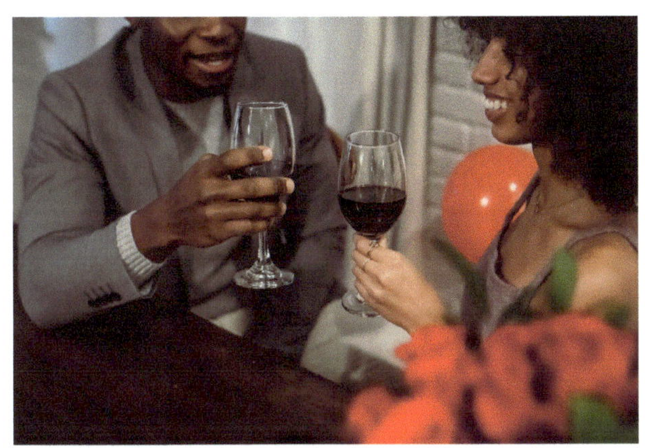

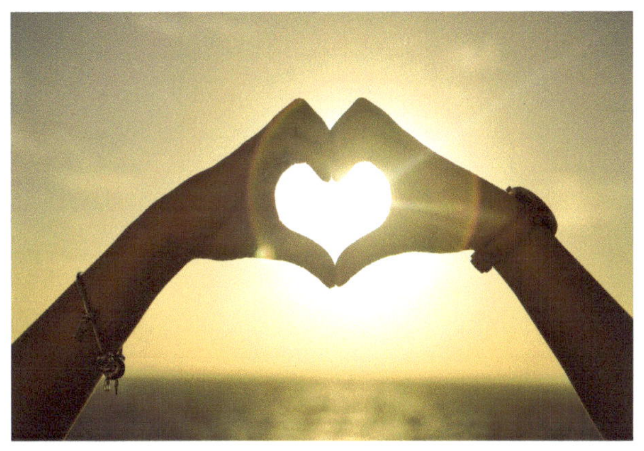

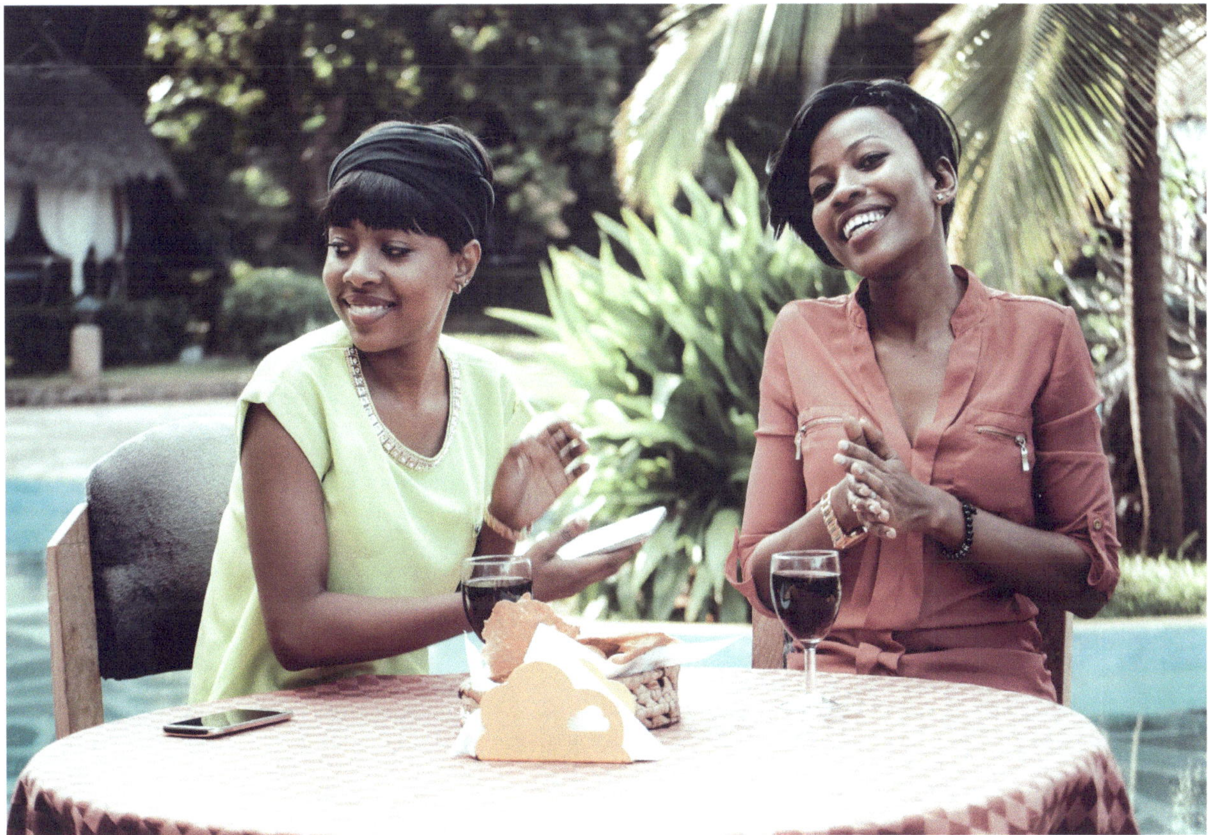

2: Family

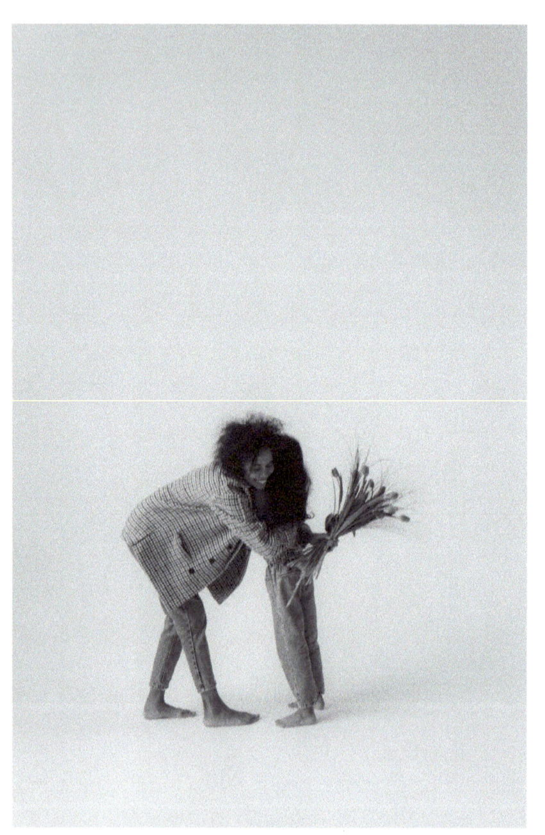

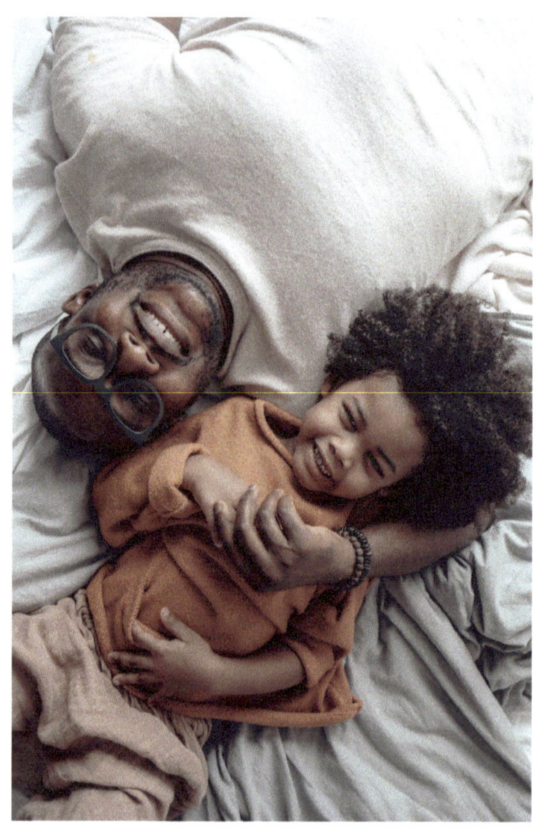

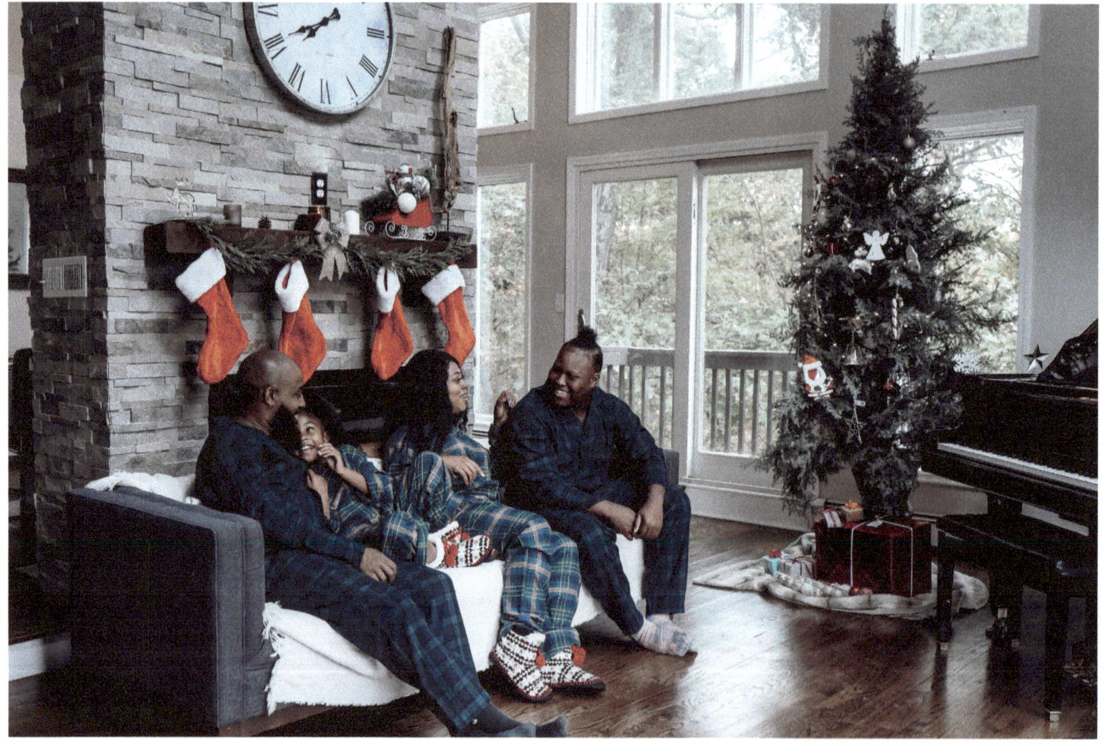

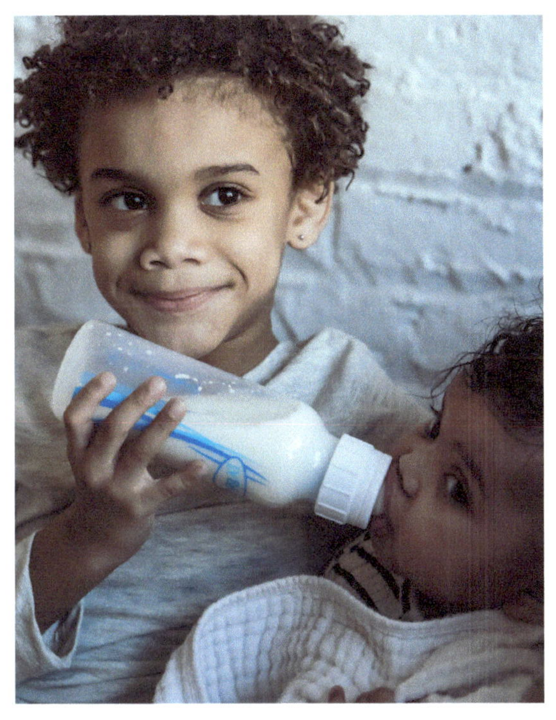
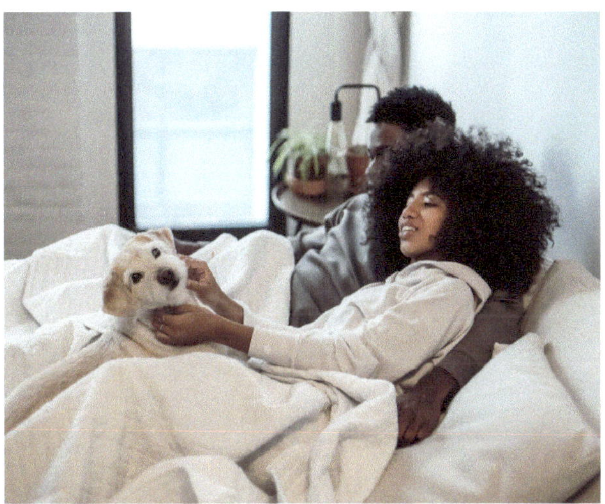
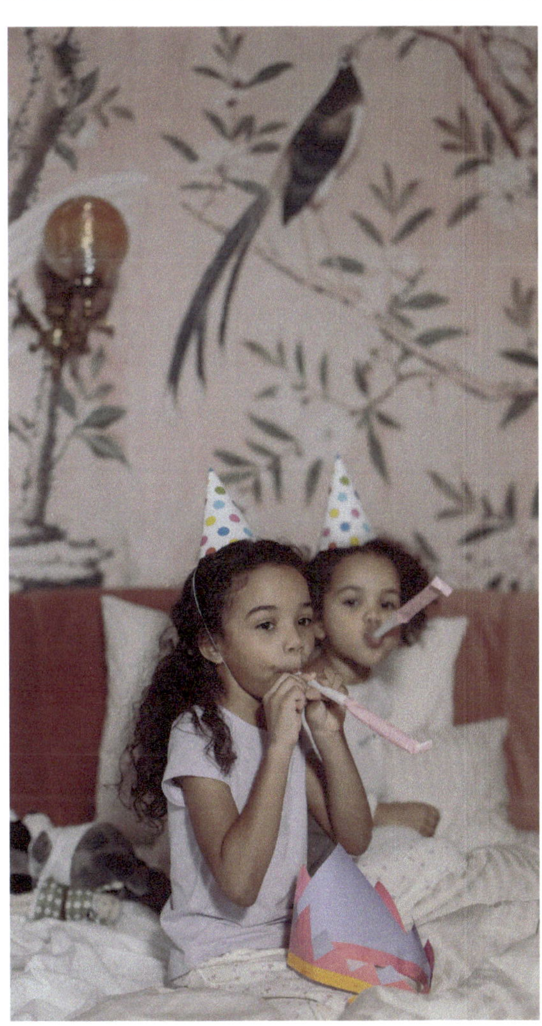
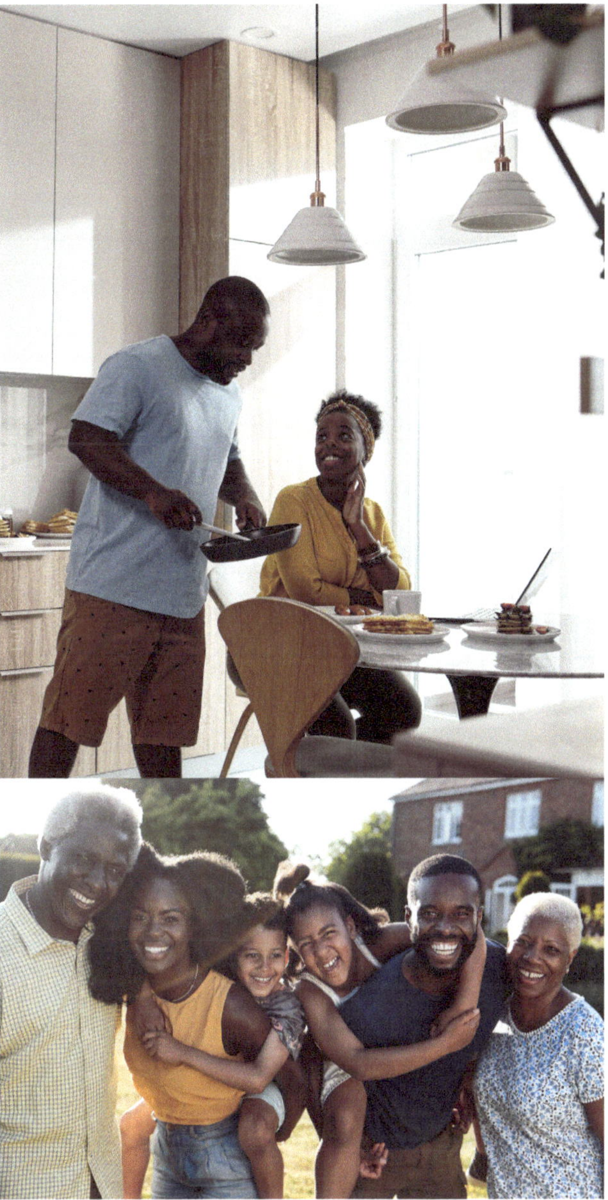

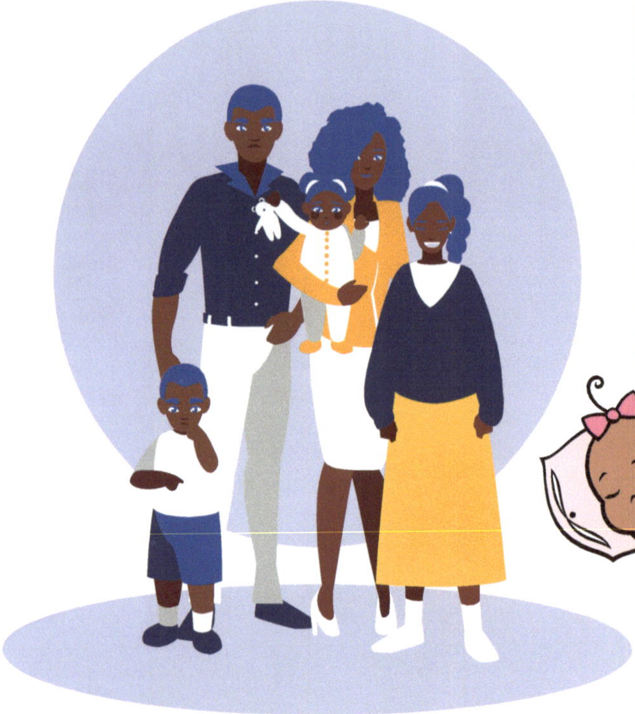

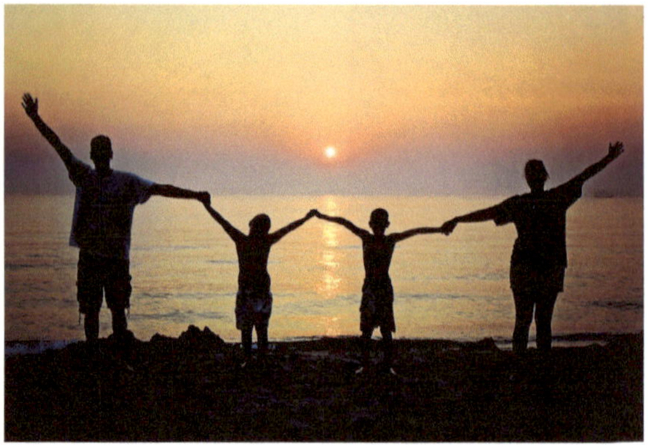

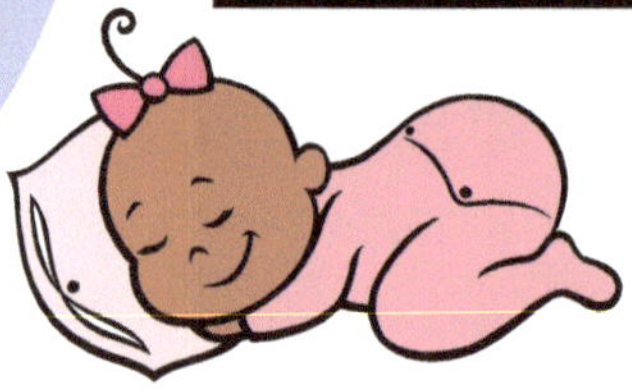

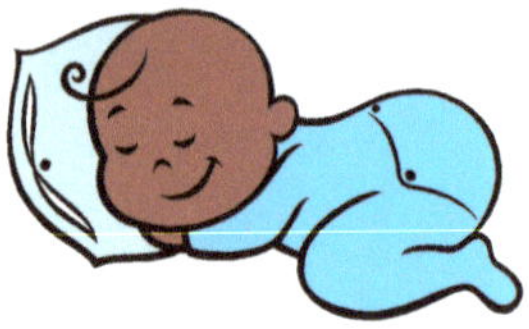

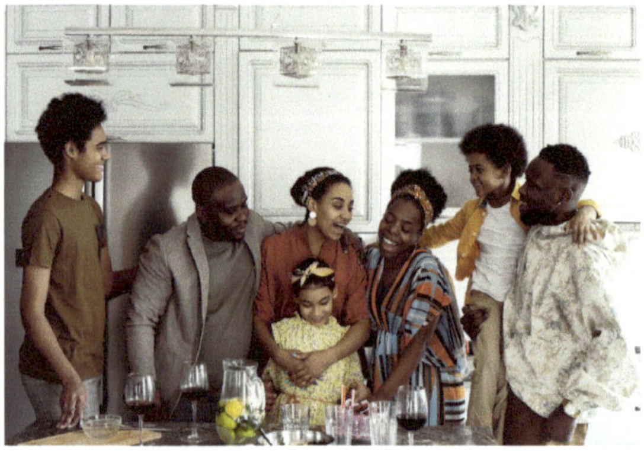

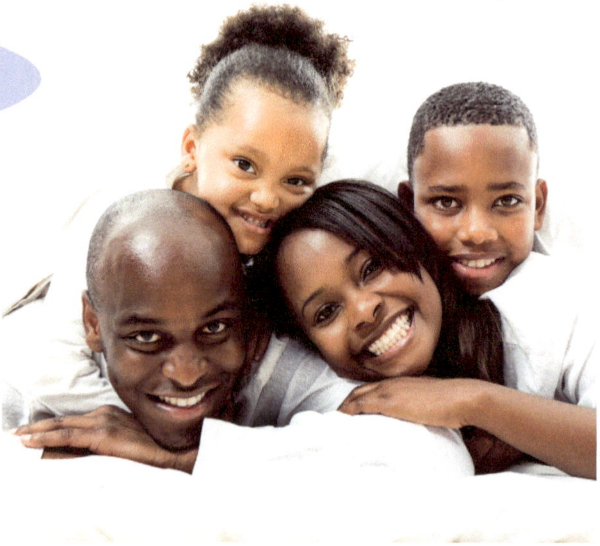

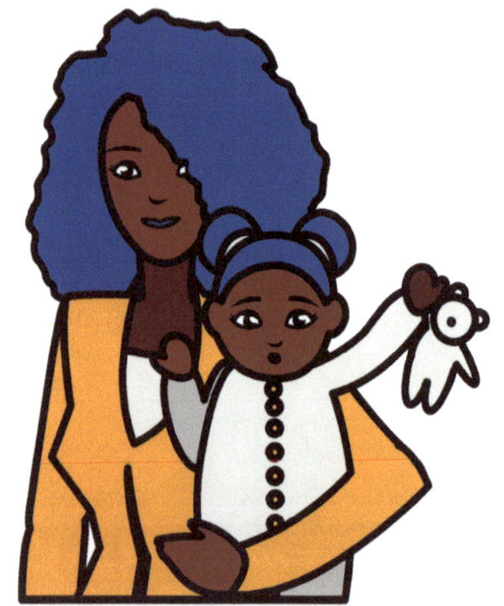
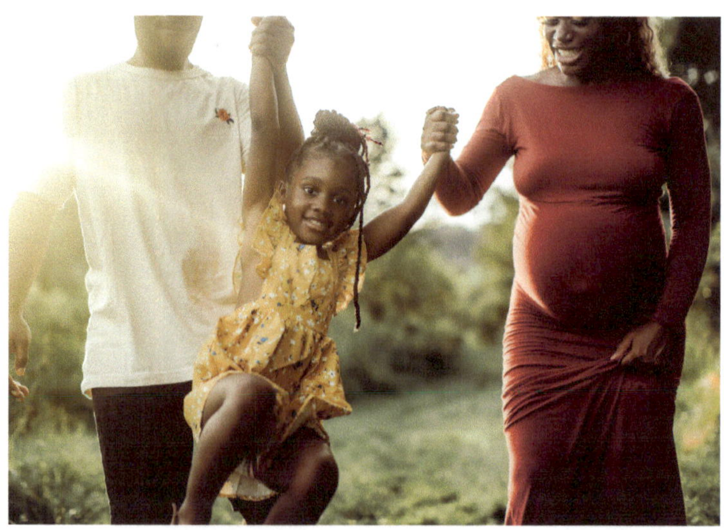

3: Wealth & Money

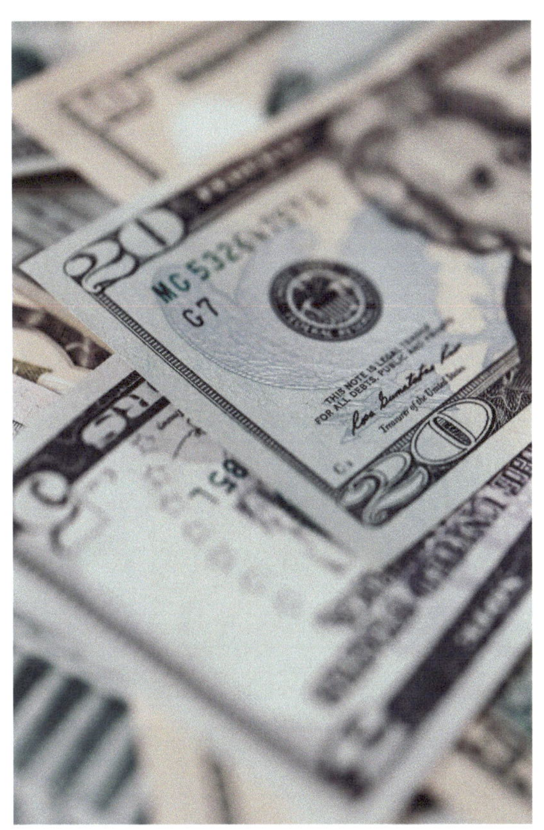
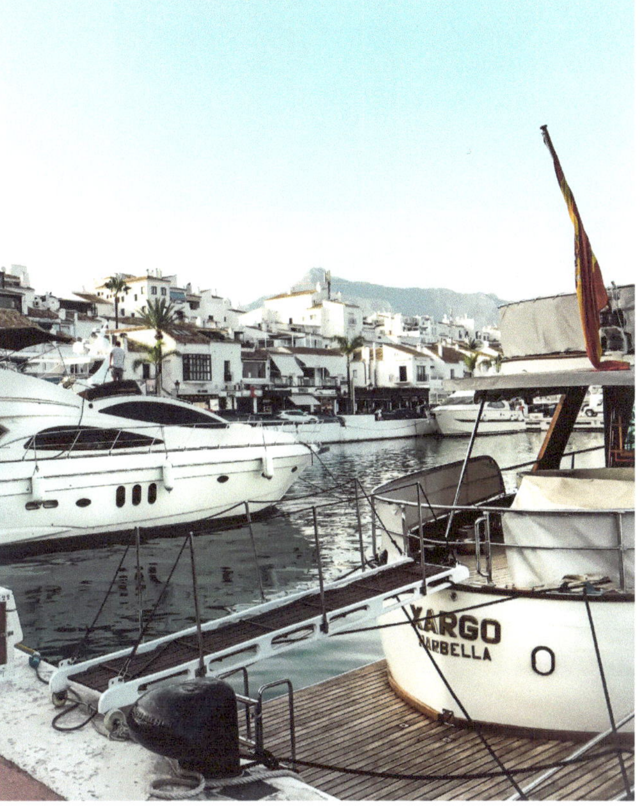
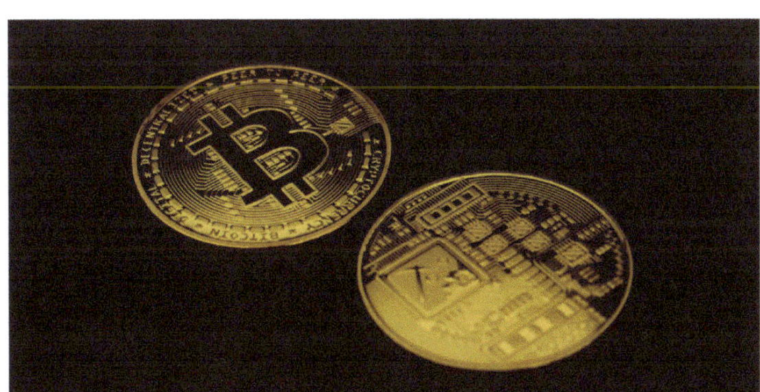
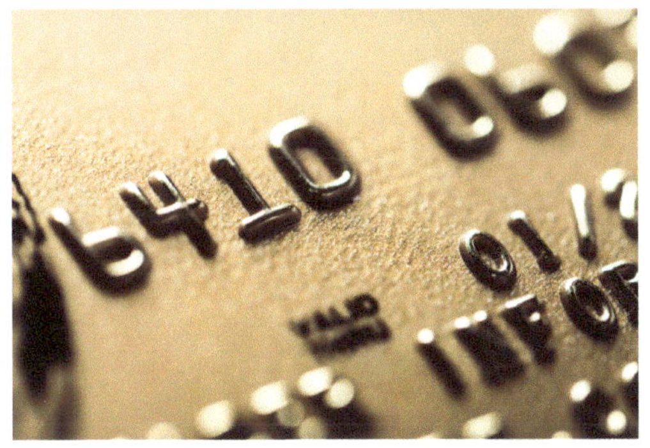
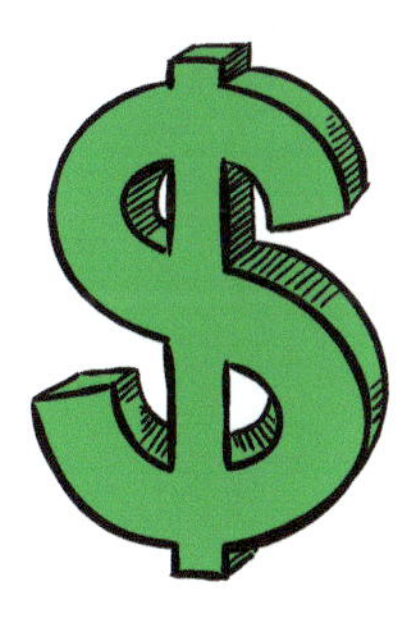
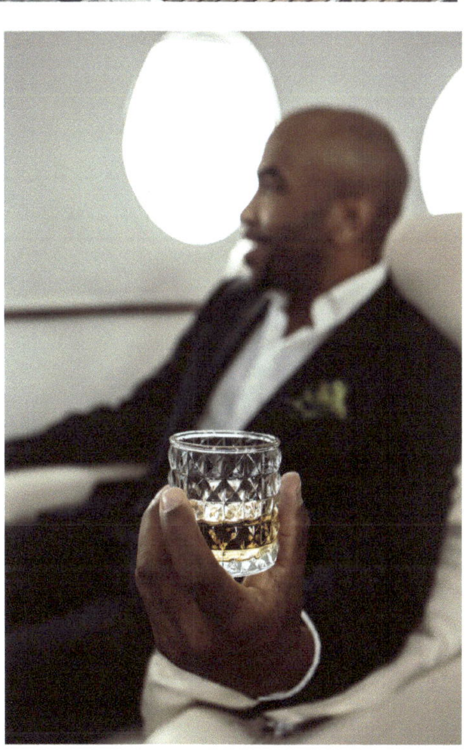

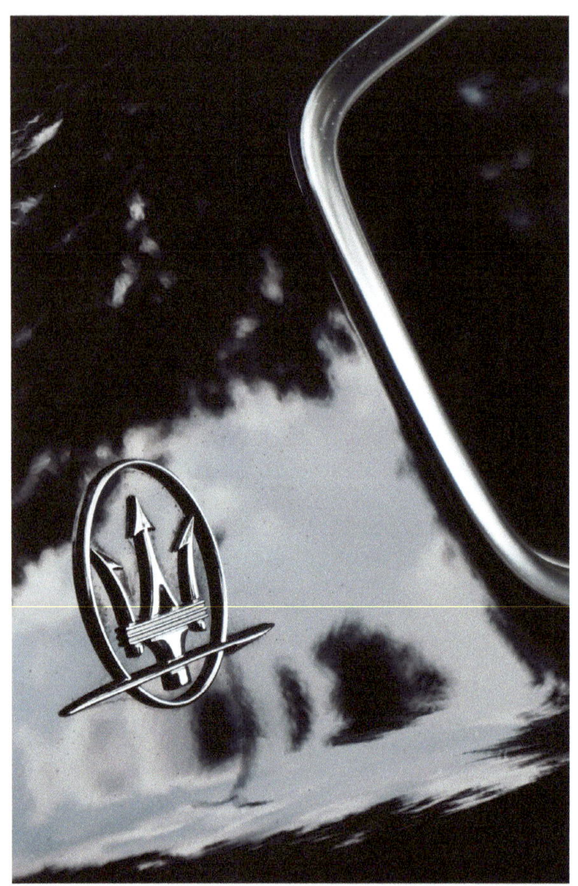

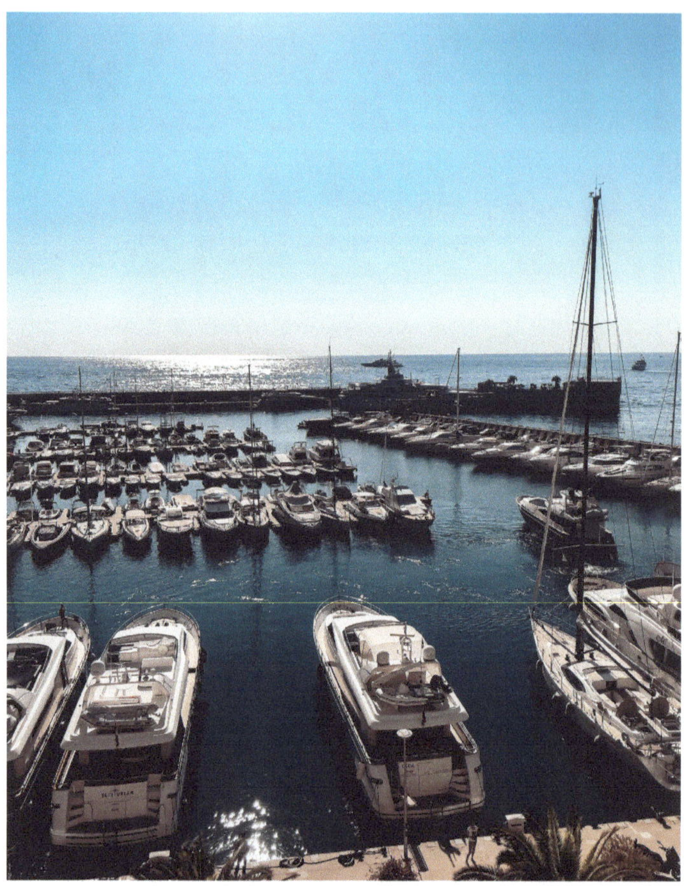

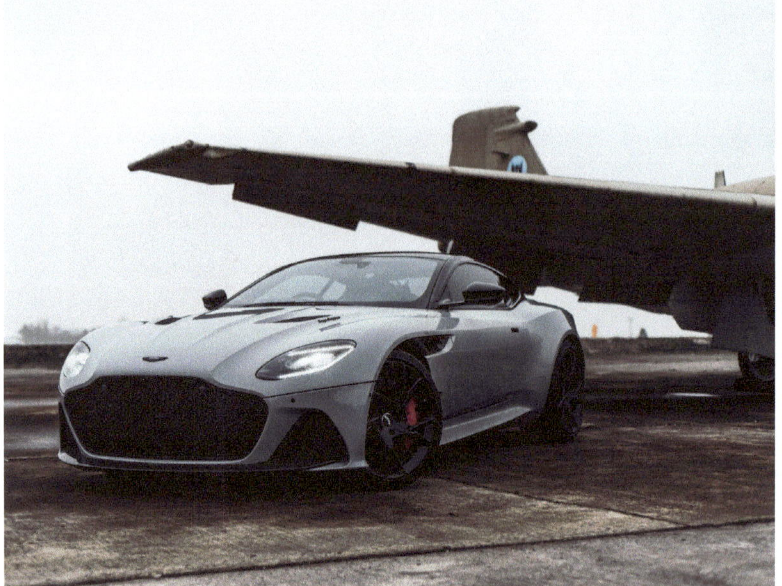

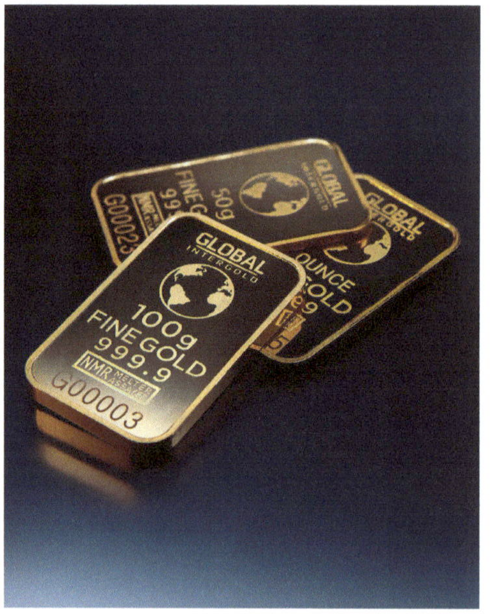

1 MILLION

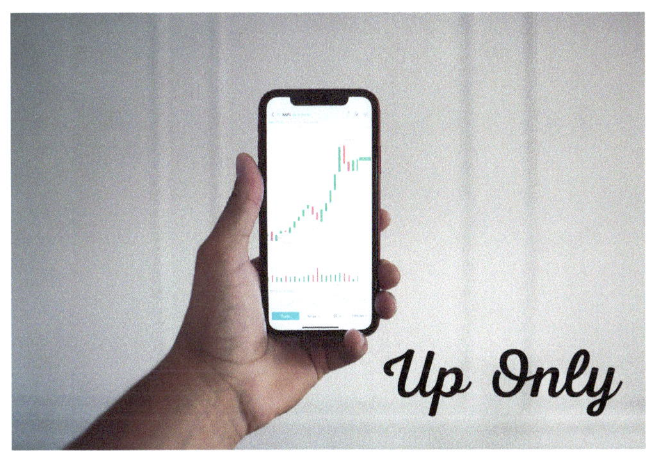
Up Only
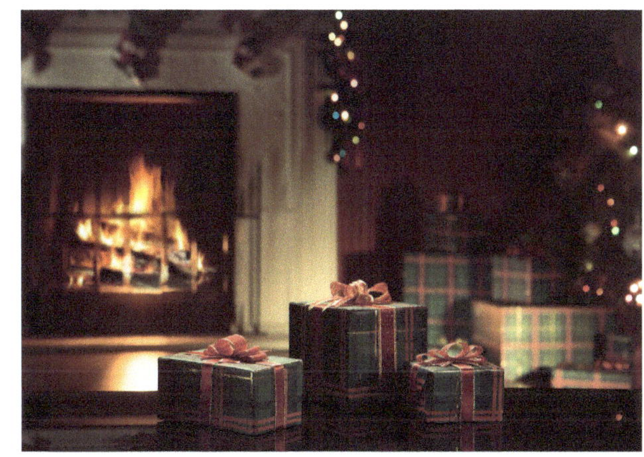
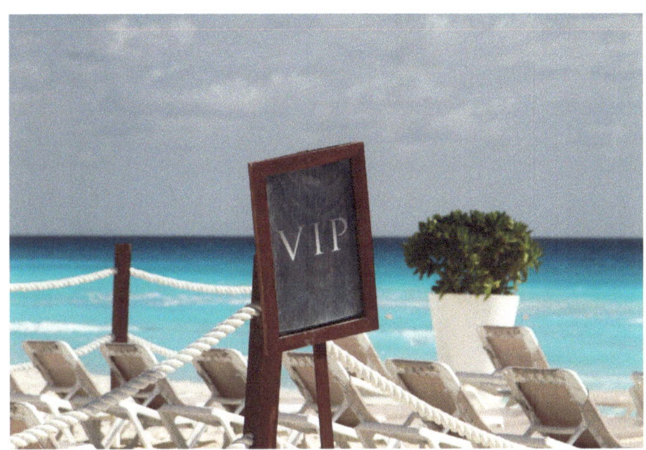
VIP
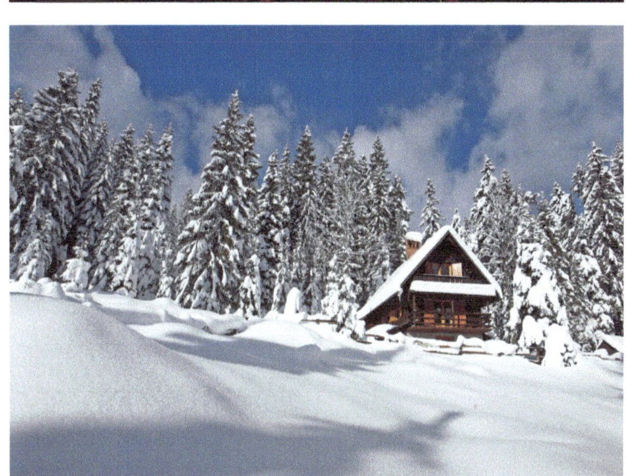
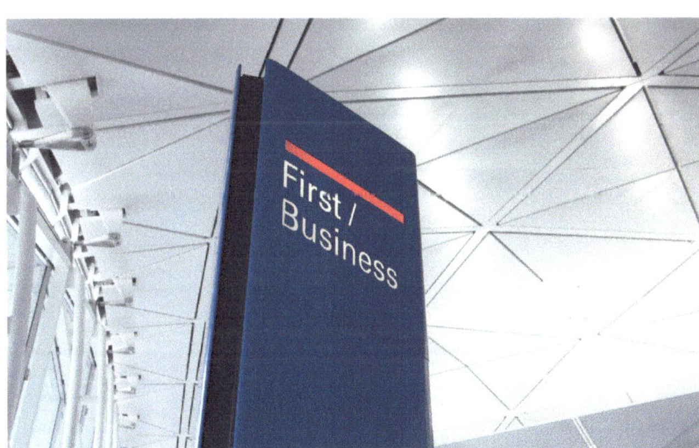
First /
Business
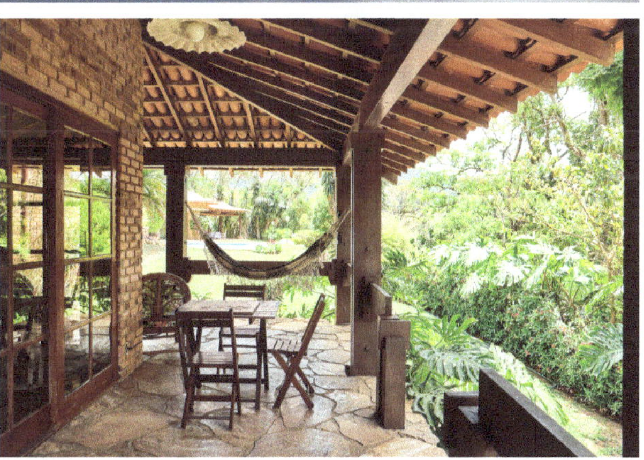
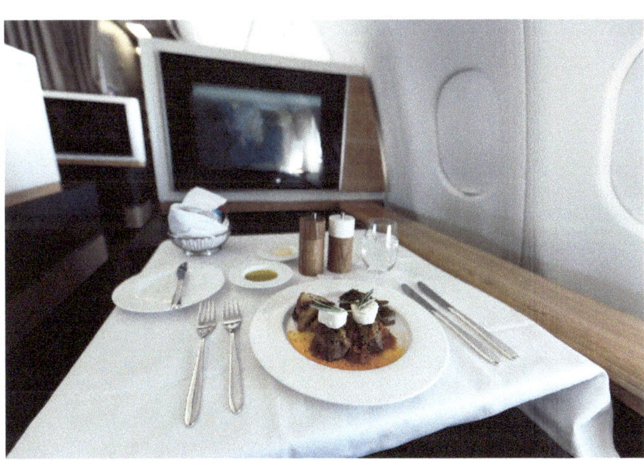
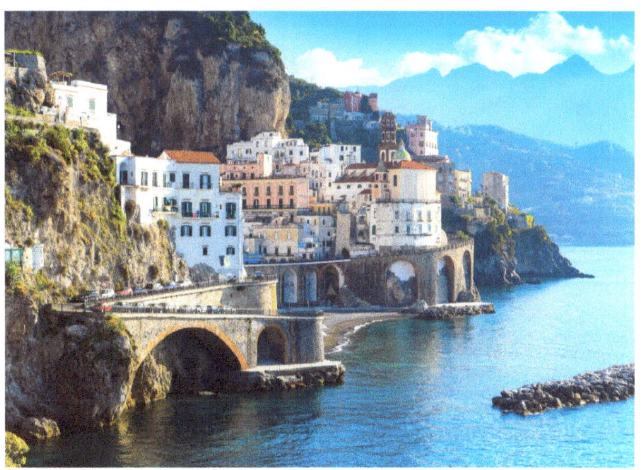

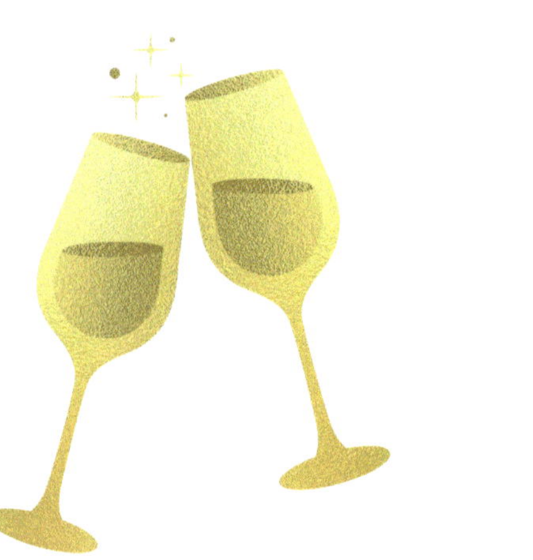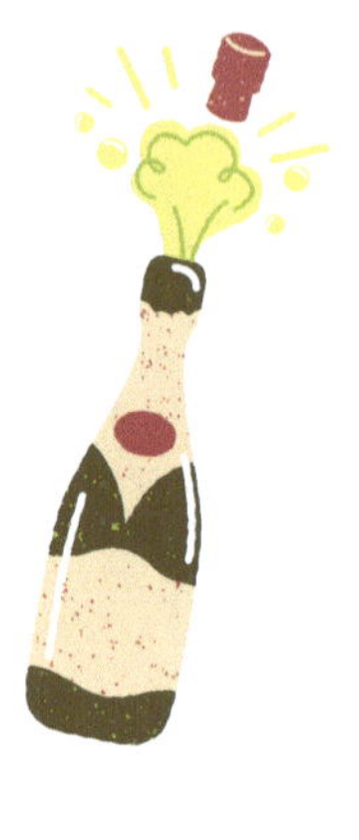

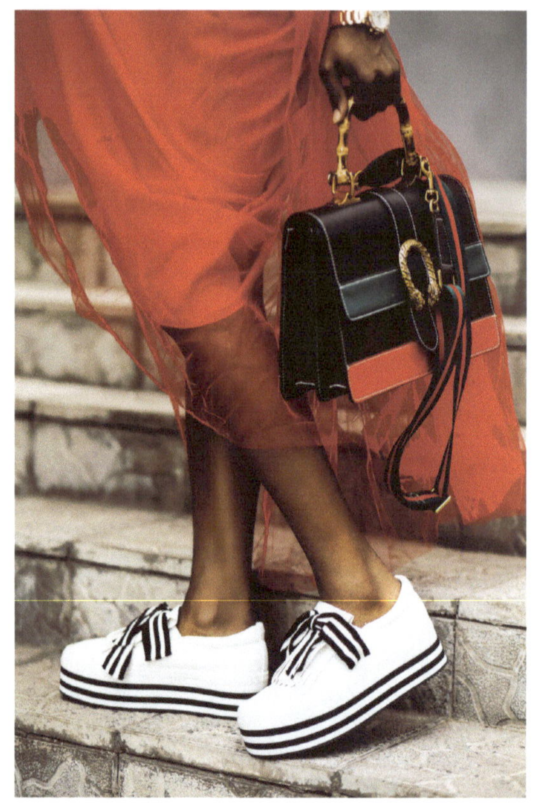

$20,000,000

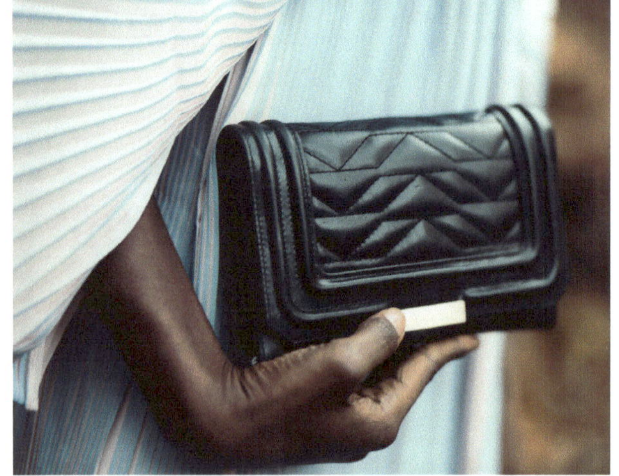

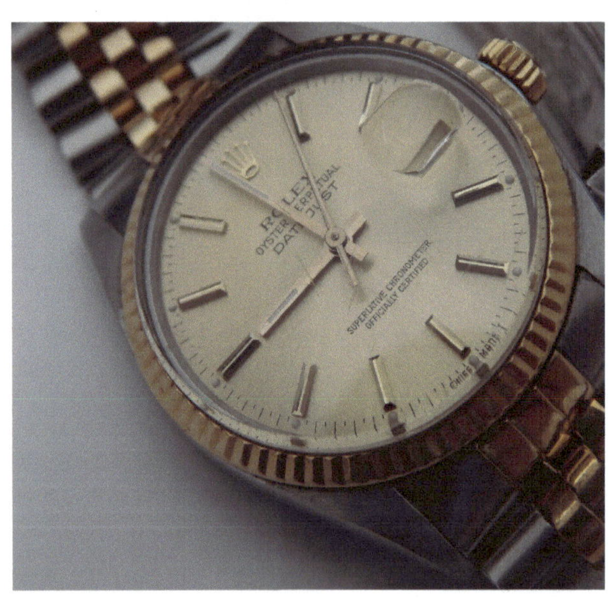

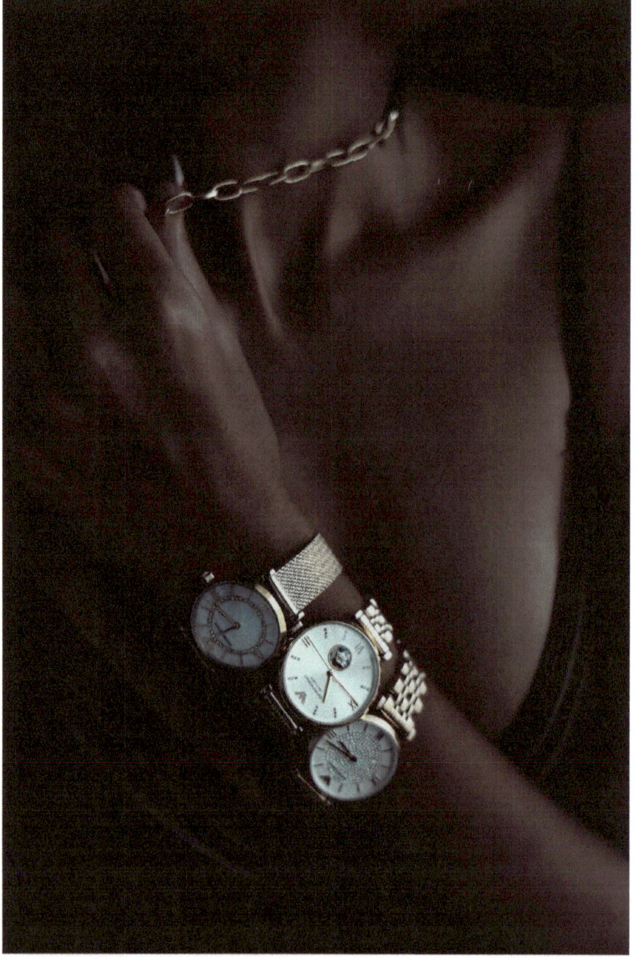

4: Business & Career

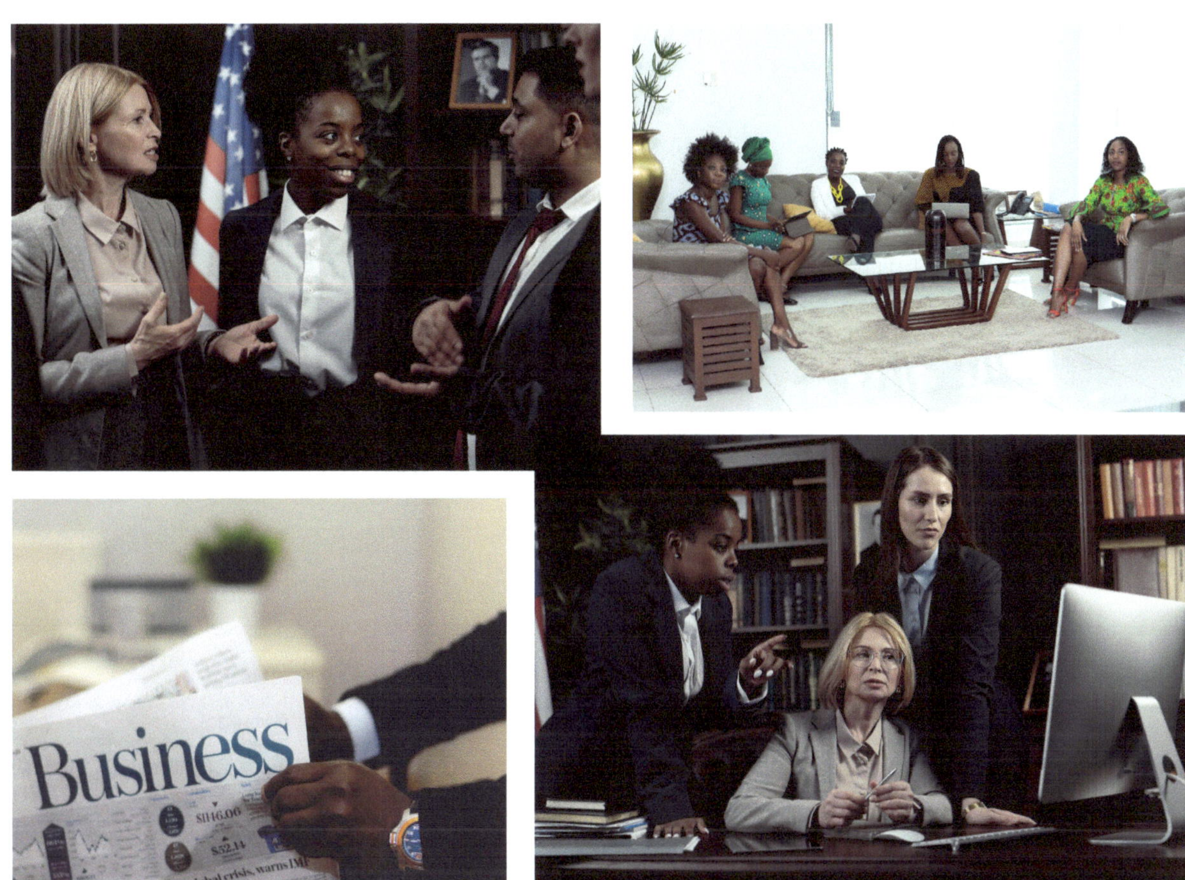

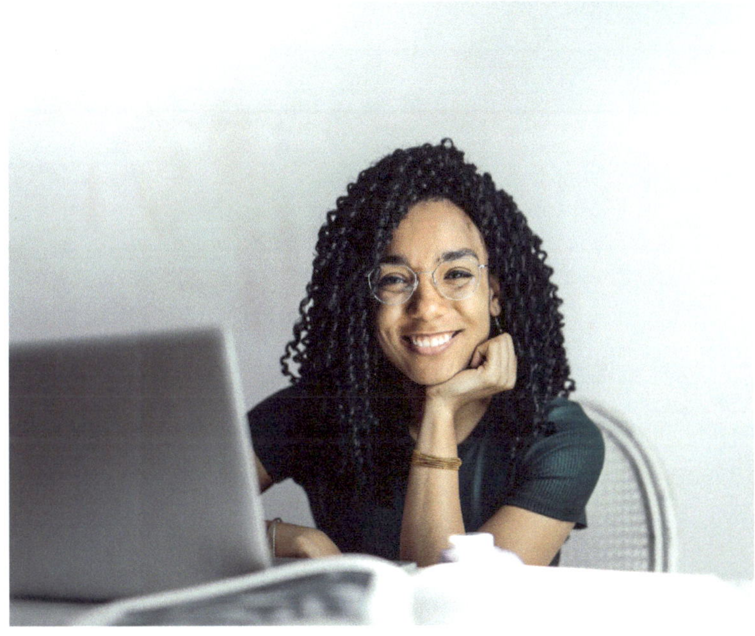

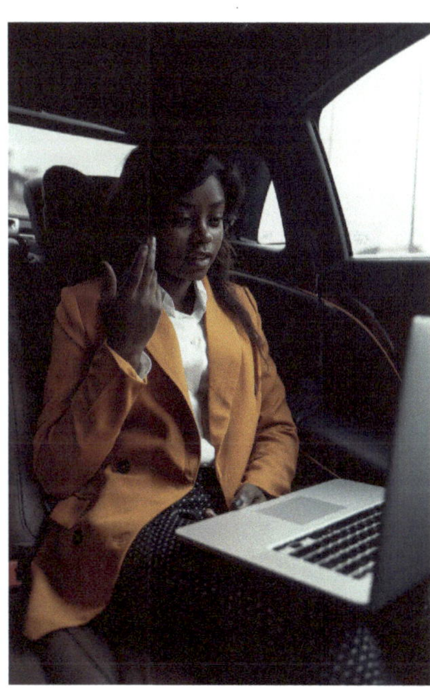

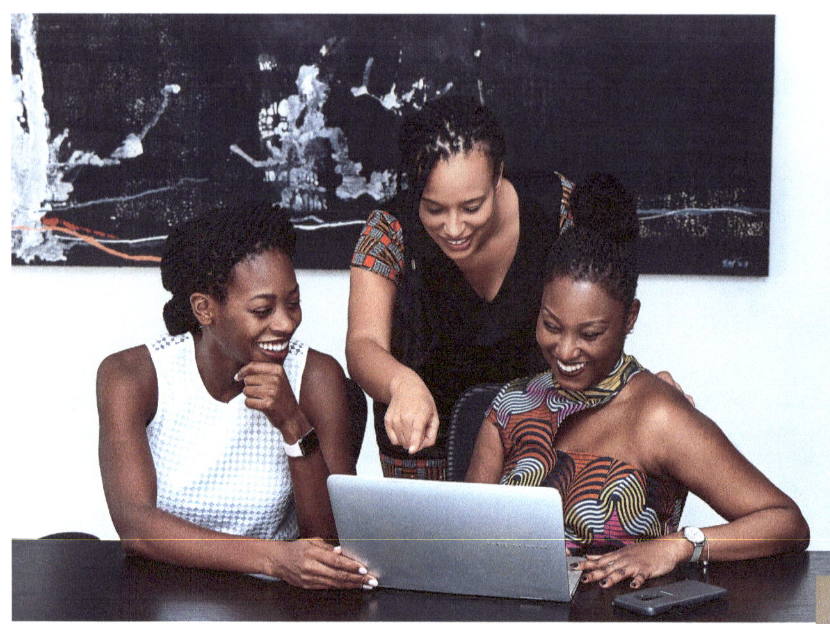
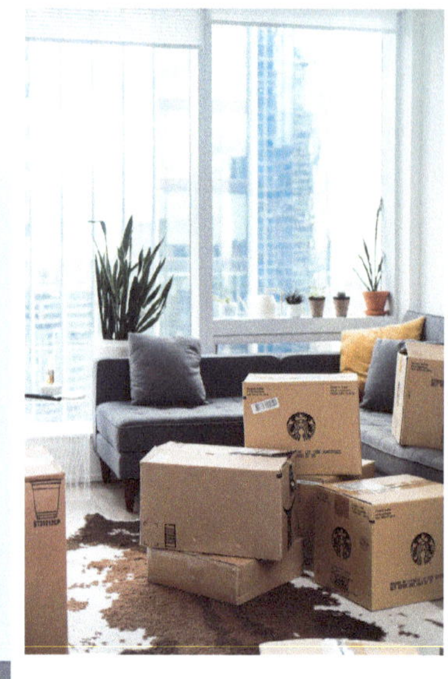
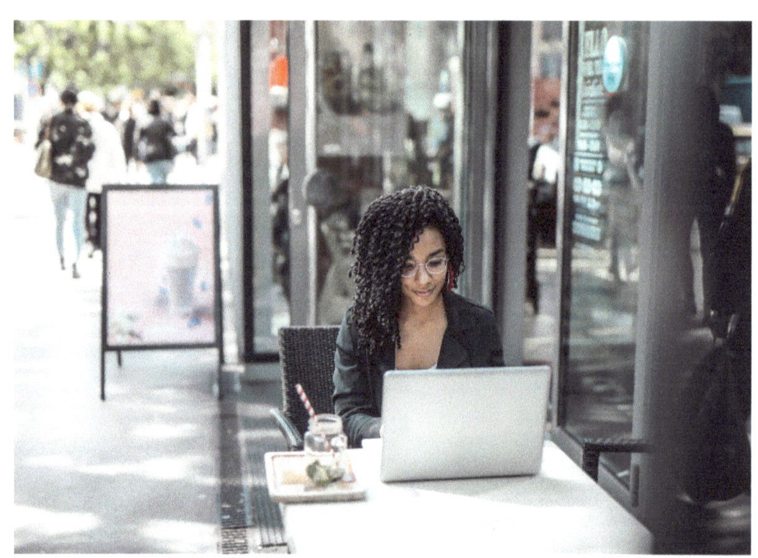
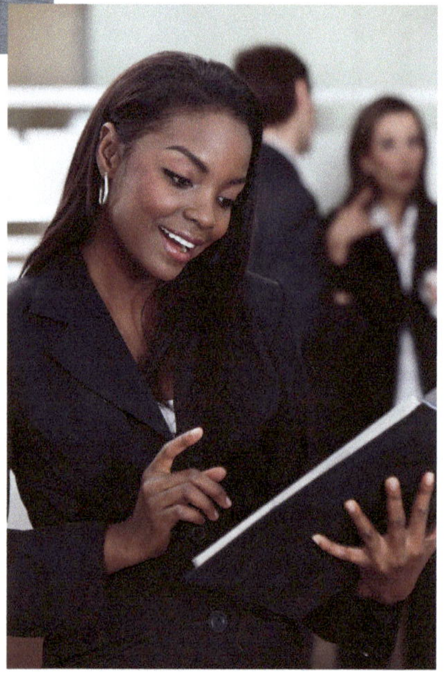
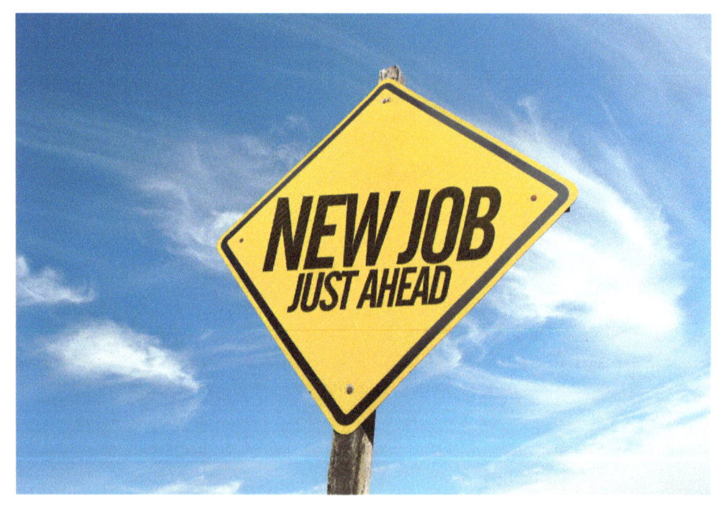

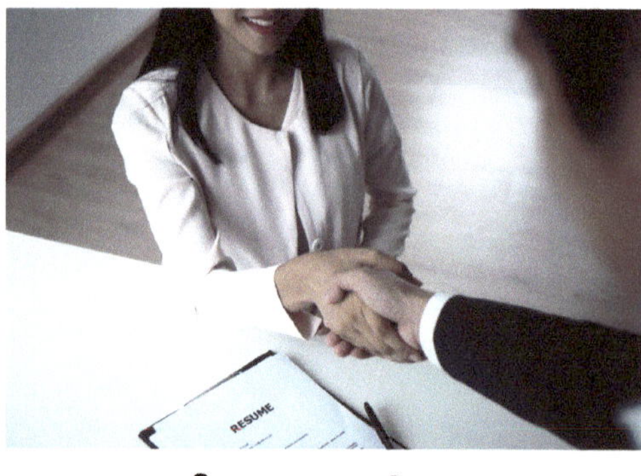

Location
Independent

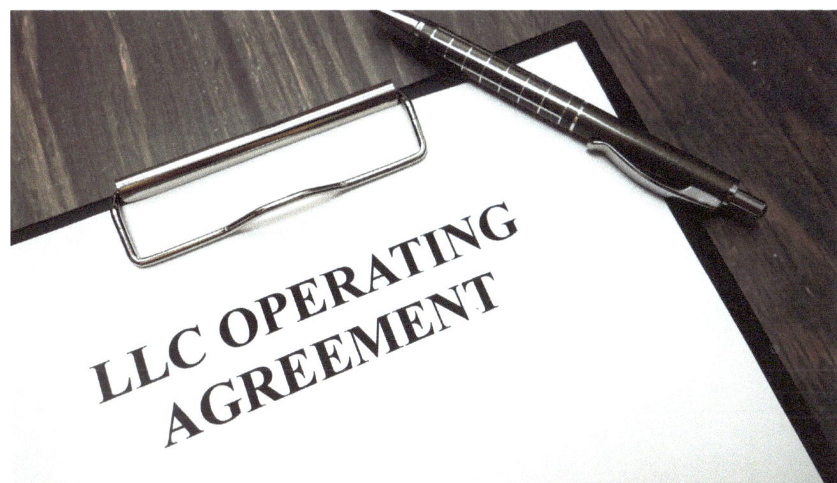

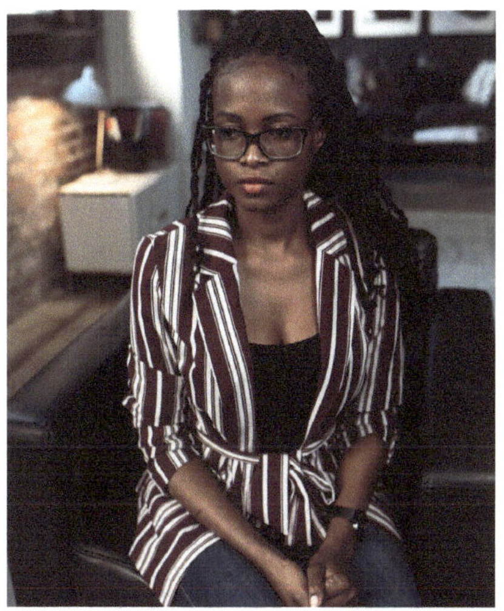

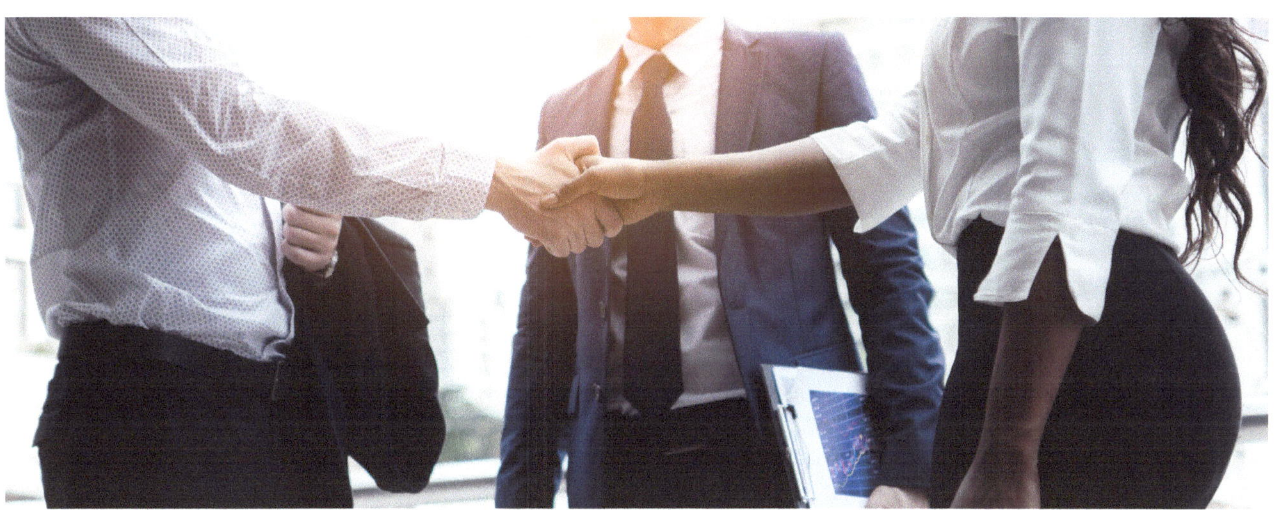

Landlady Life Wins Only

Effortless Wealth

OWNERSHIP

5: Spirituality / God

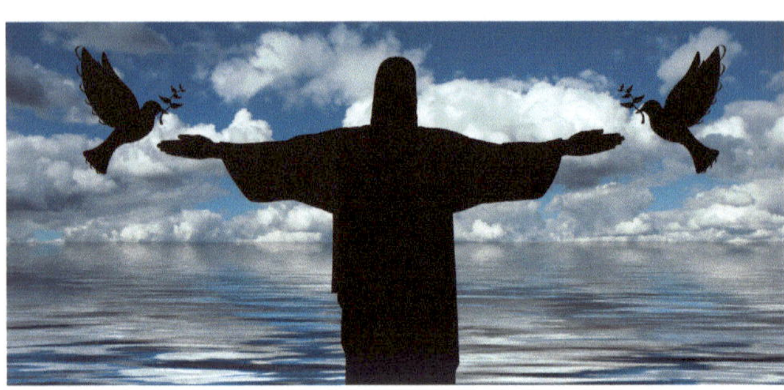

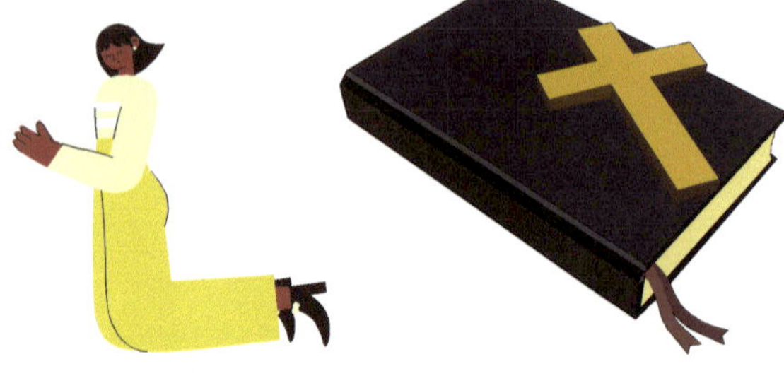

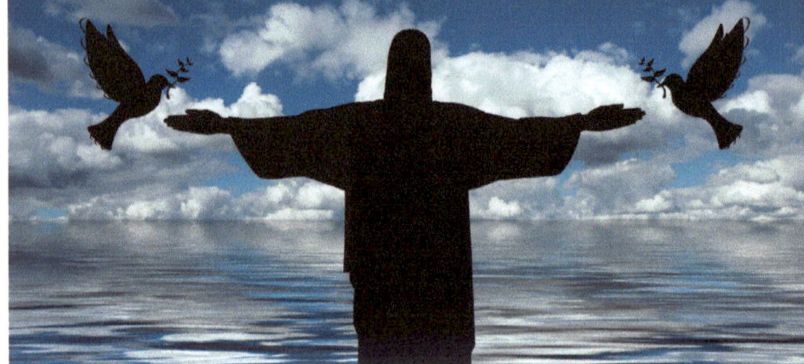

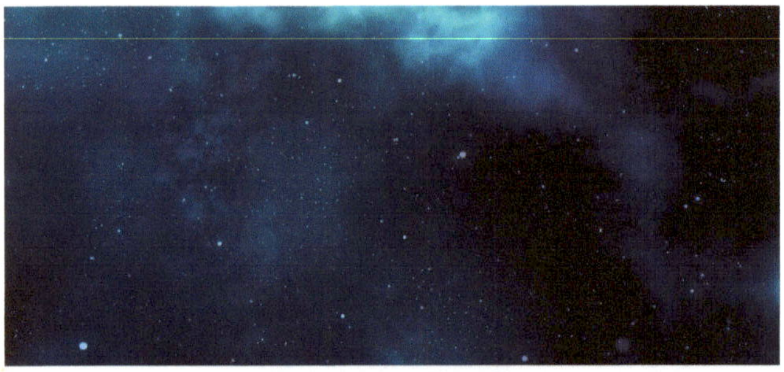

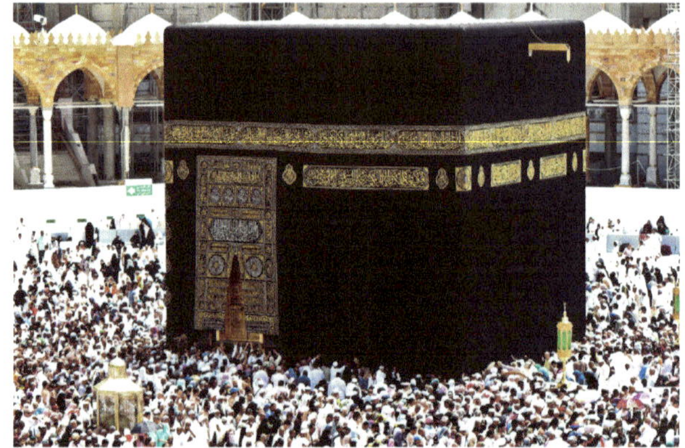

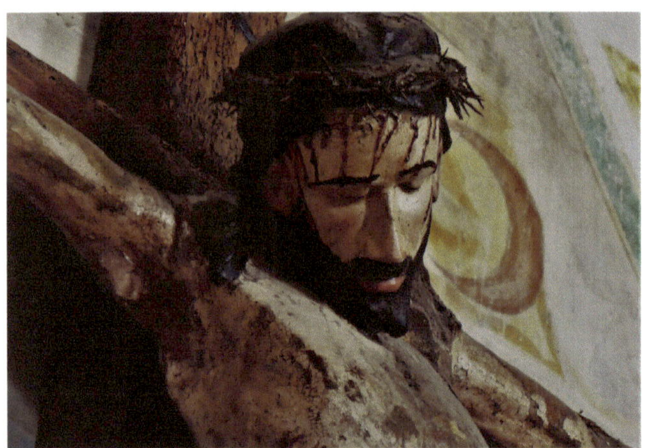

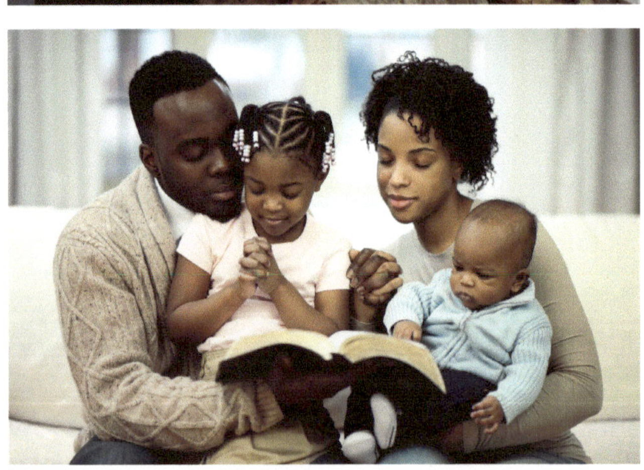

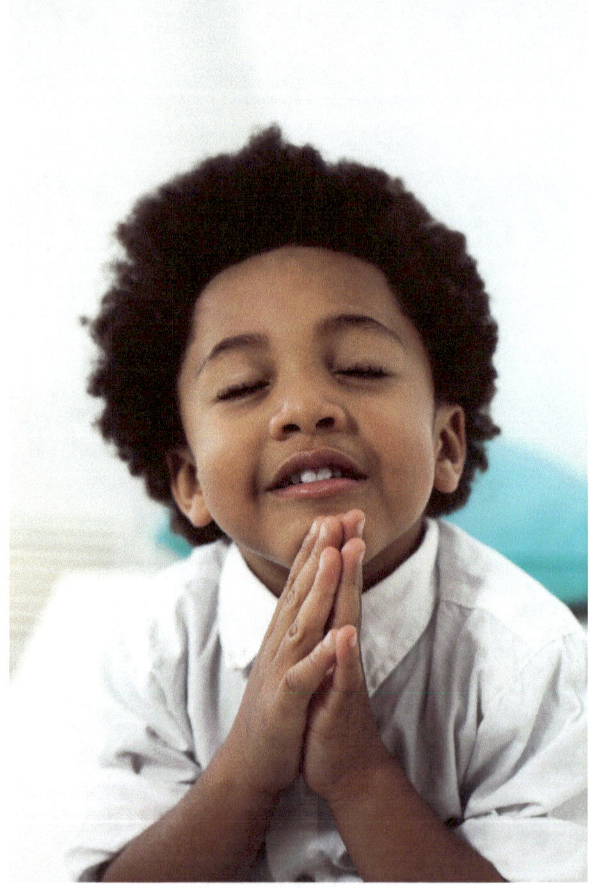

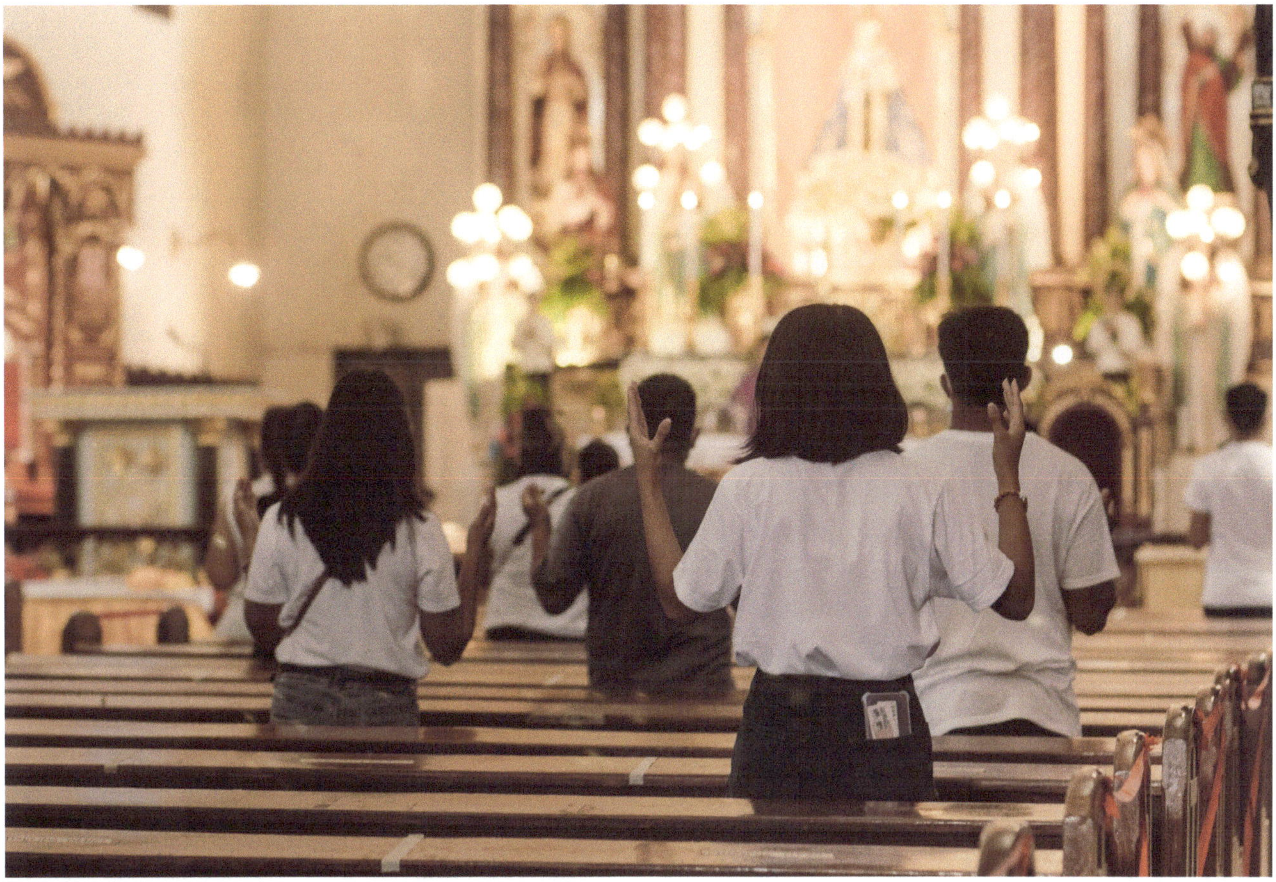

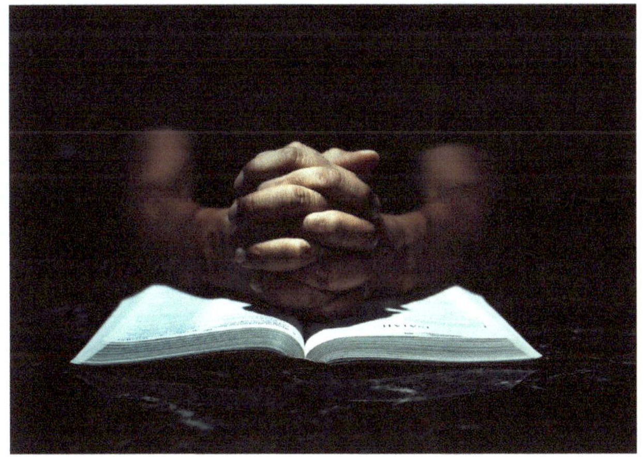

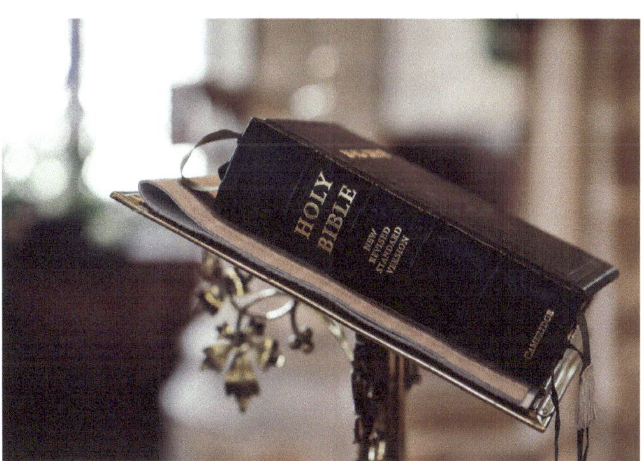

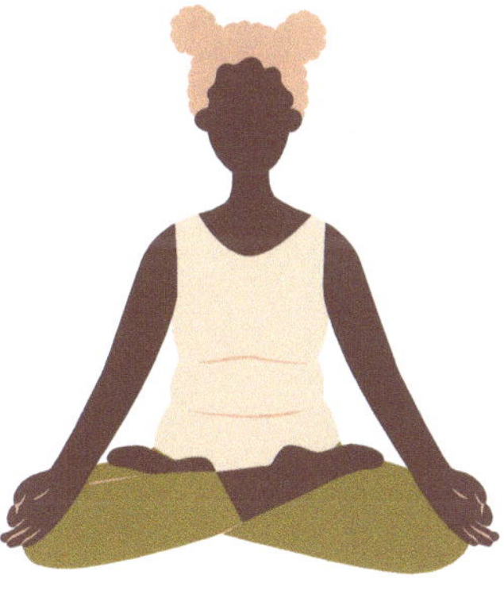

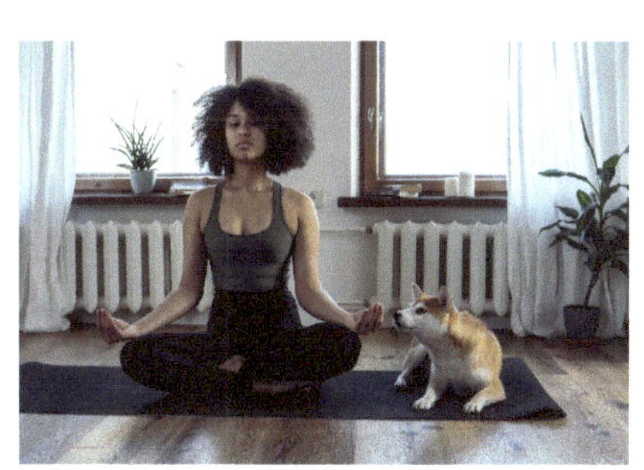

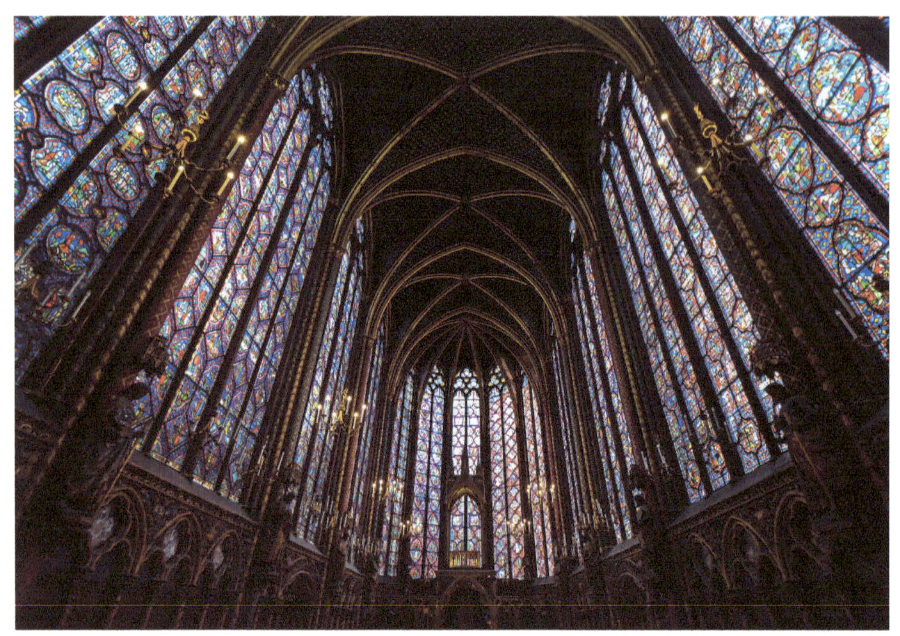
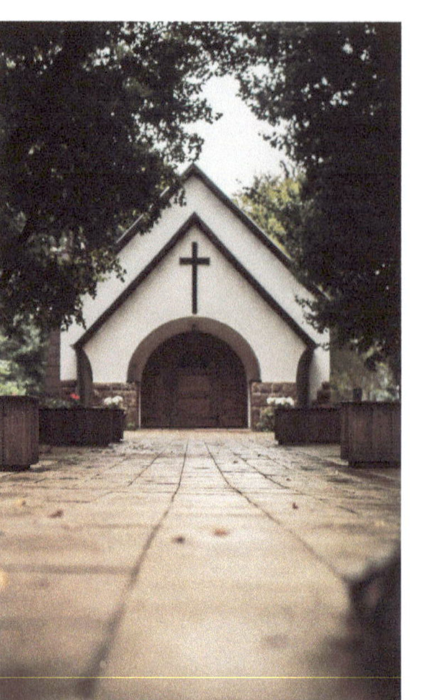
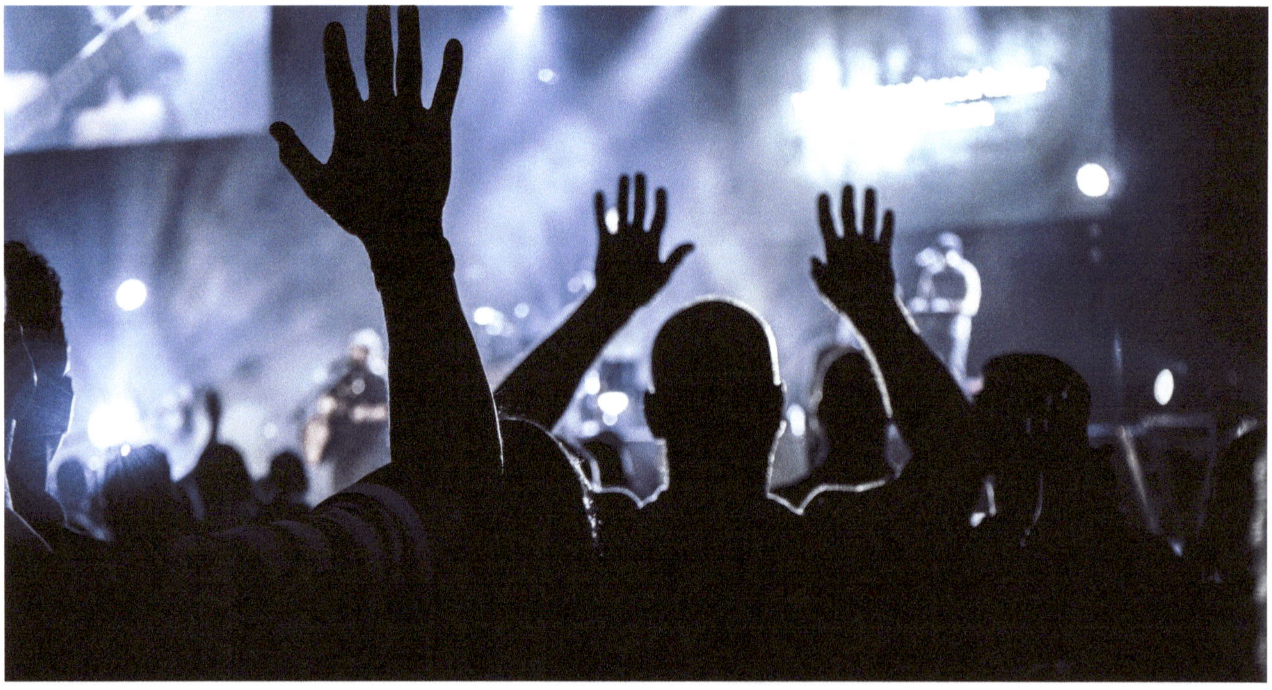
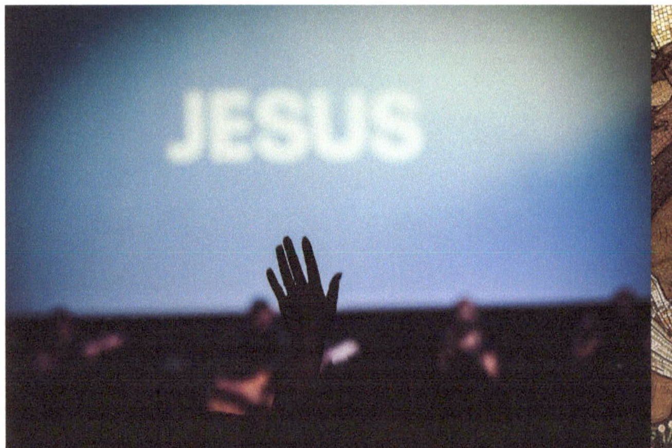
JESUS
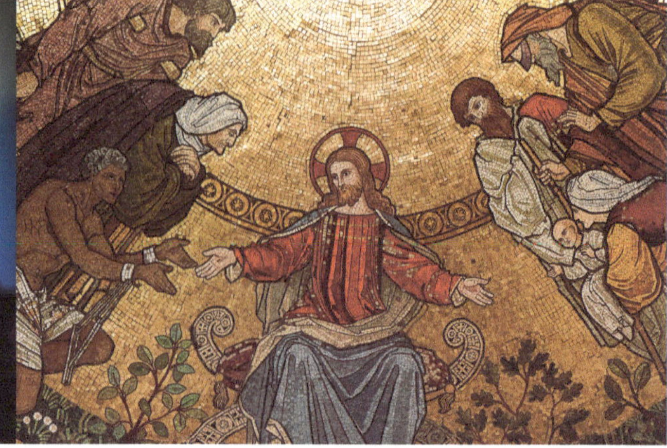

6: New House & Land

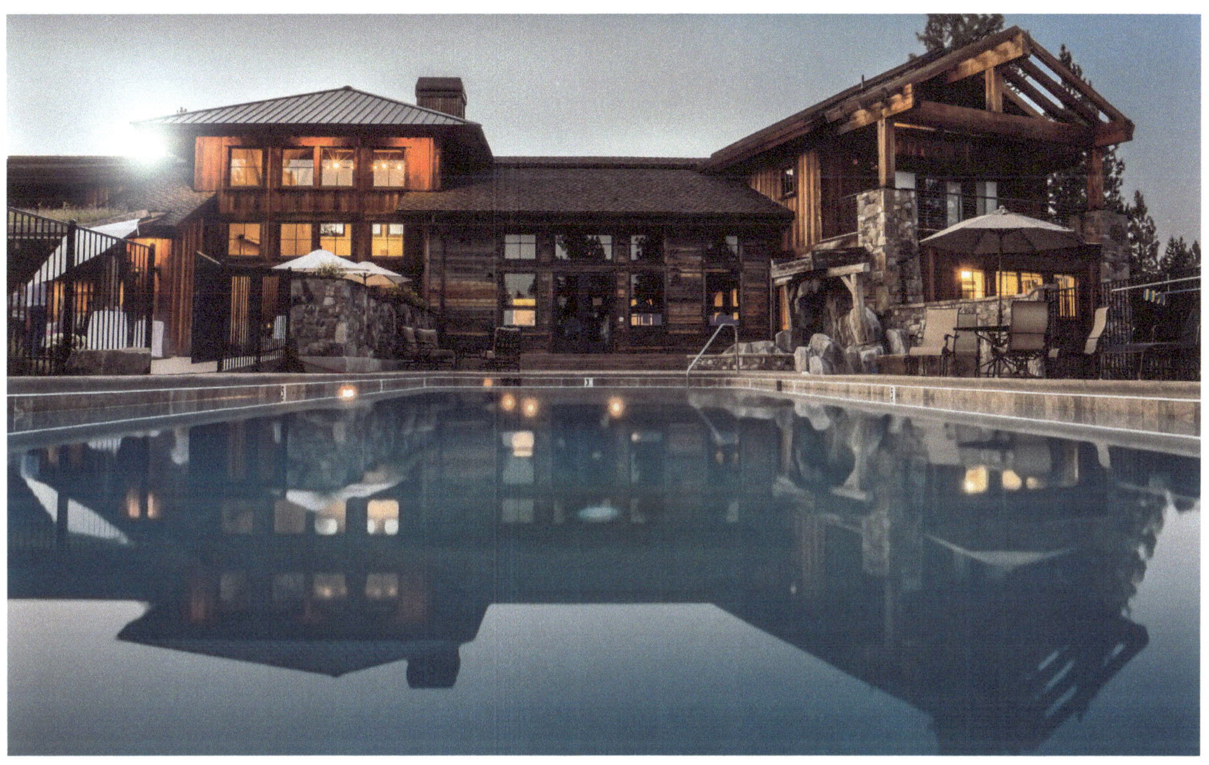

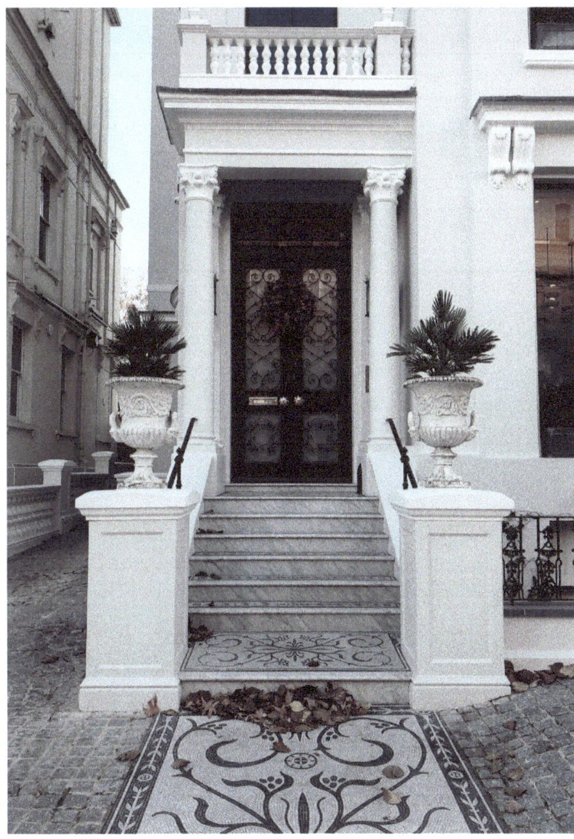

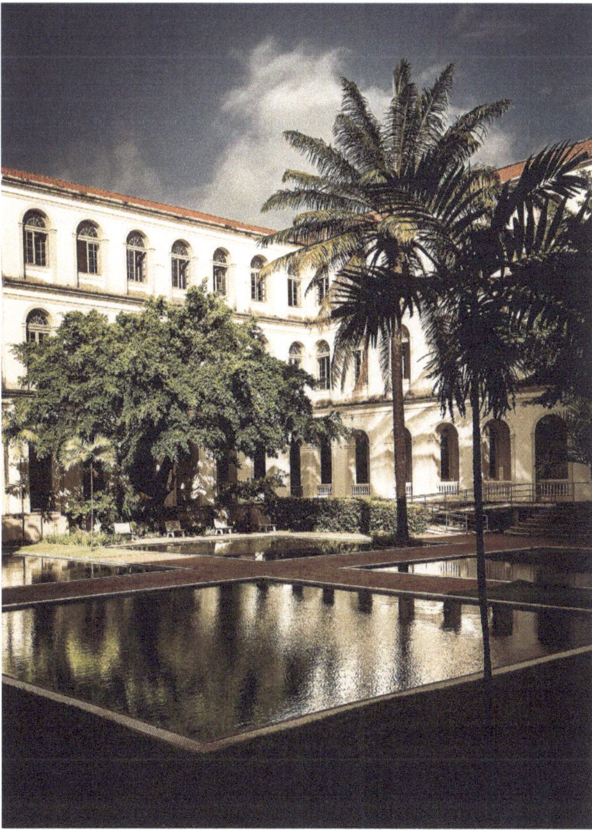

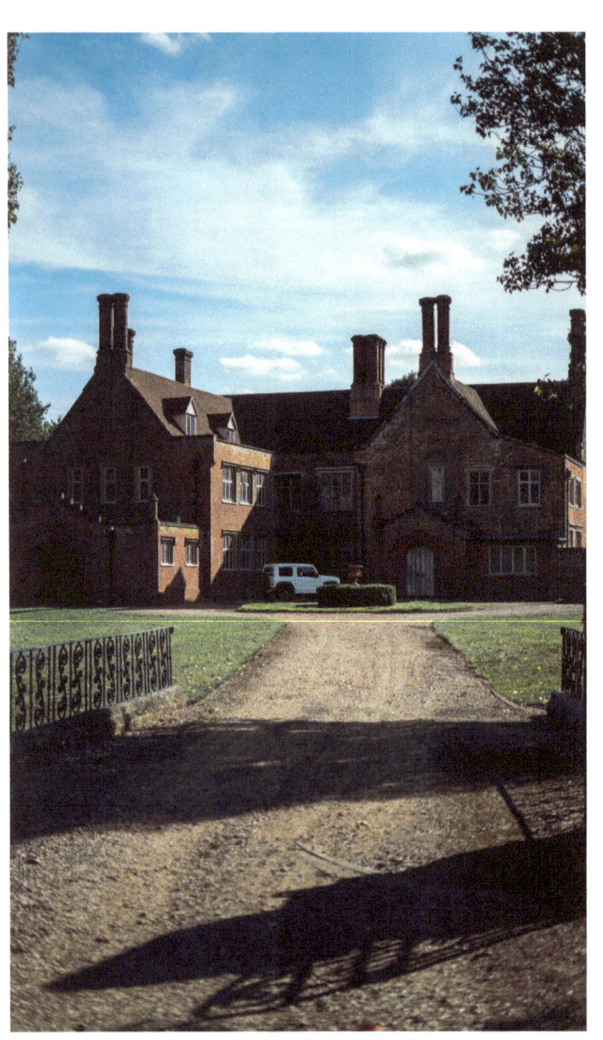
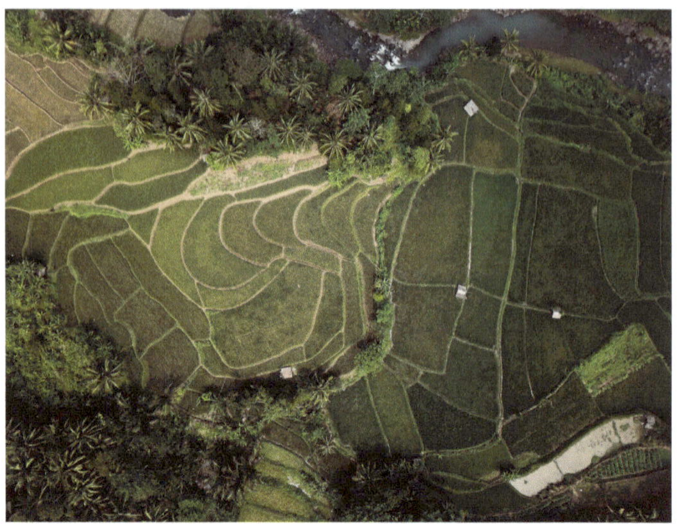
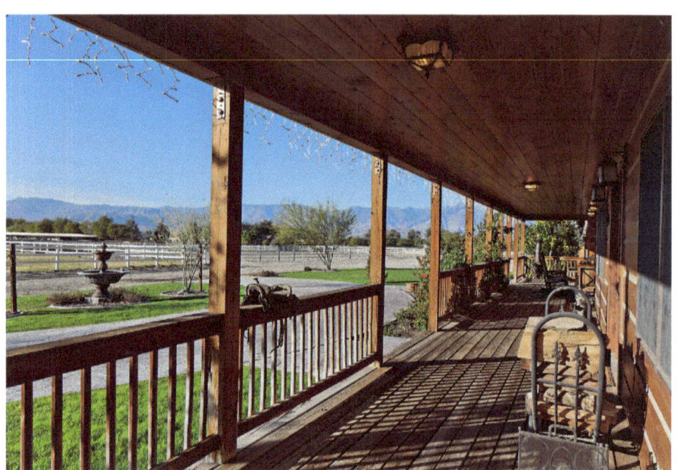
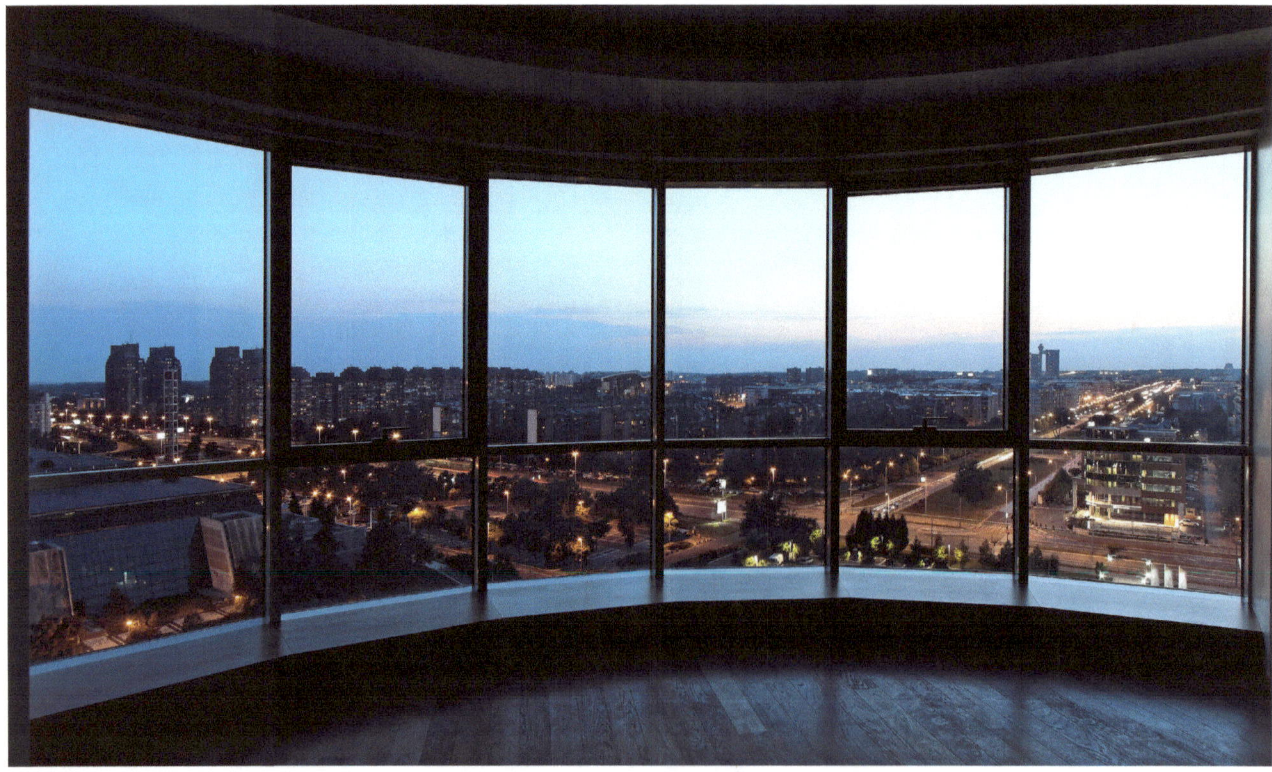

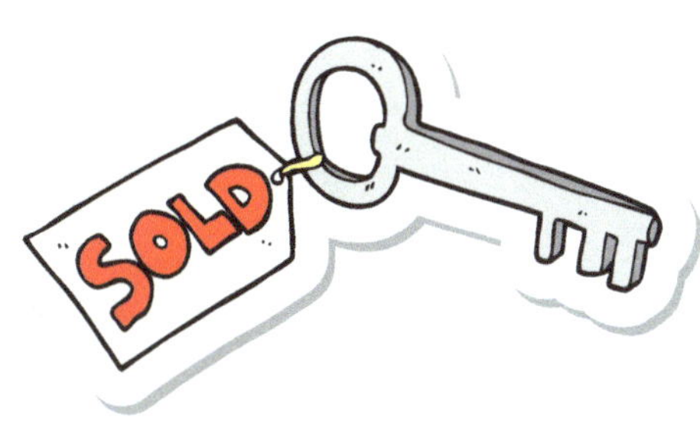
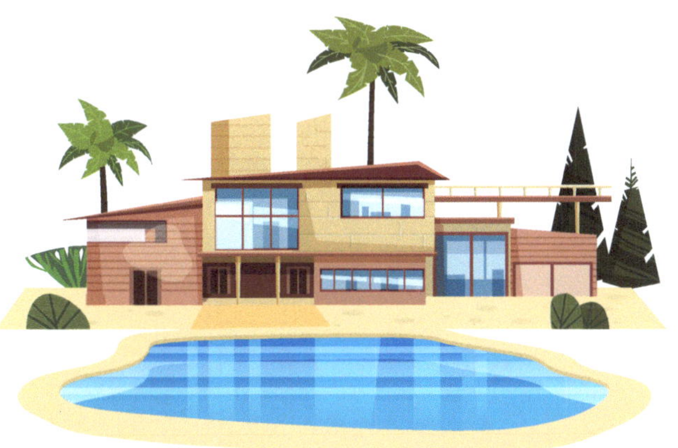
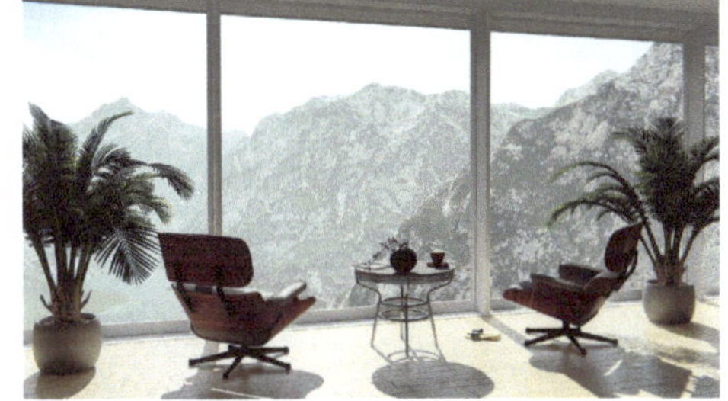
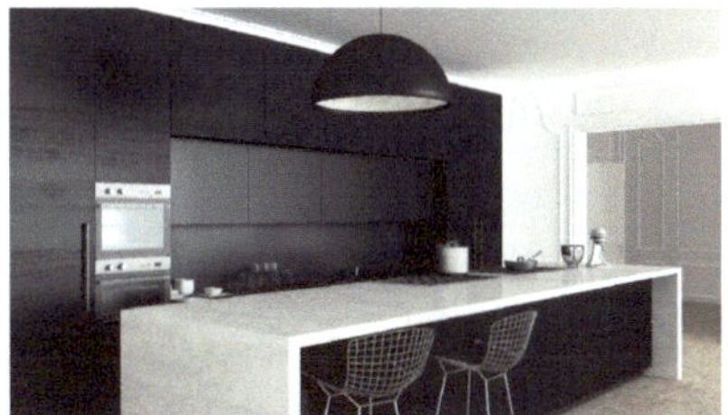
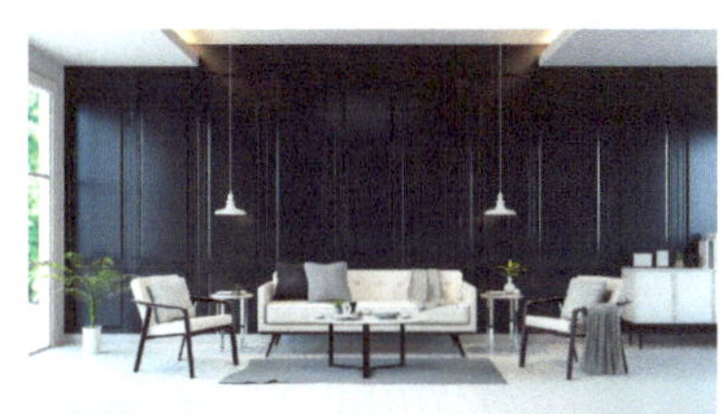
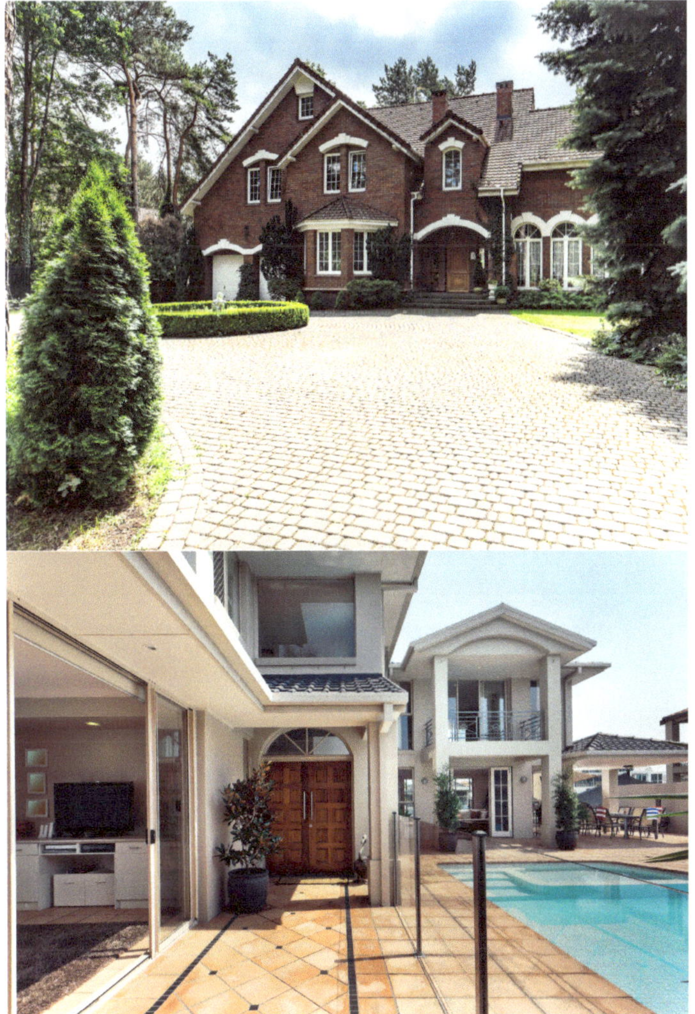
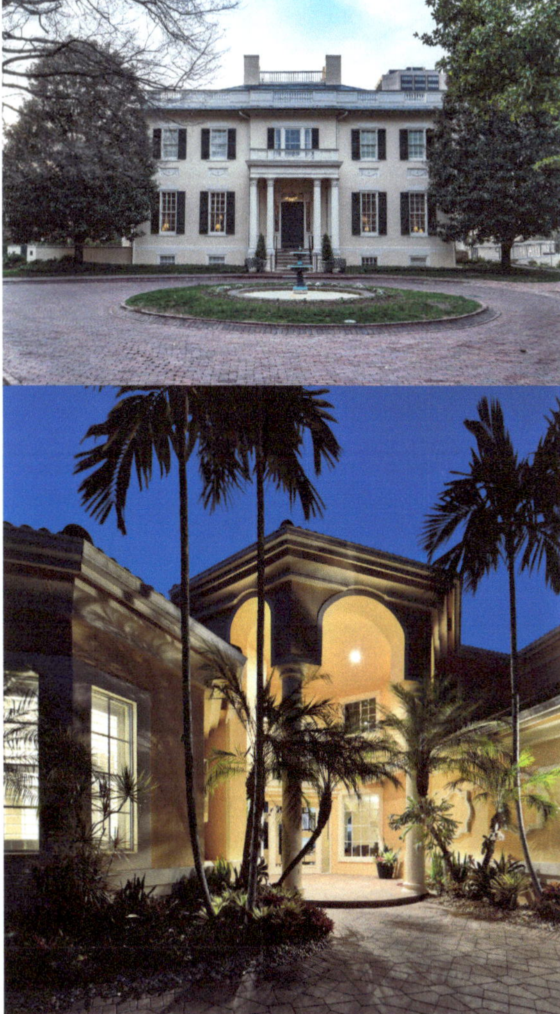

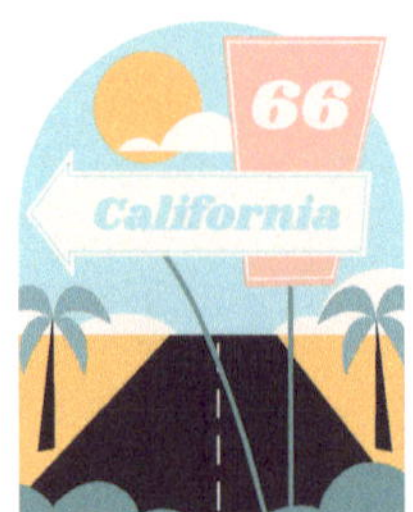
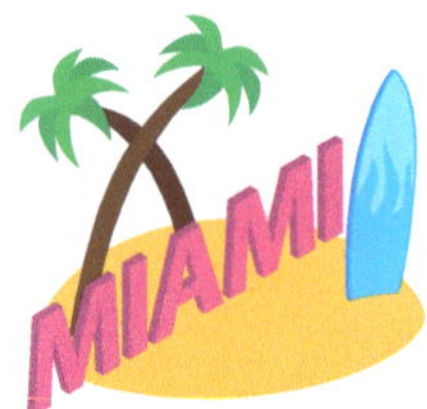
66
California
MIAMI
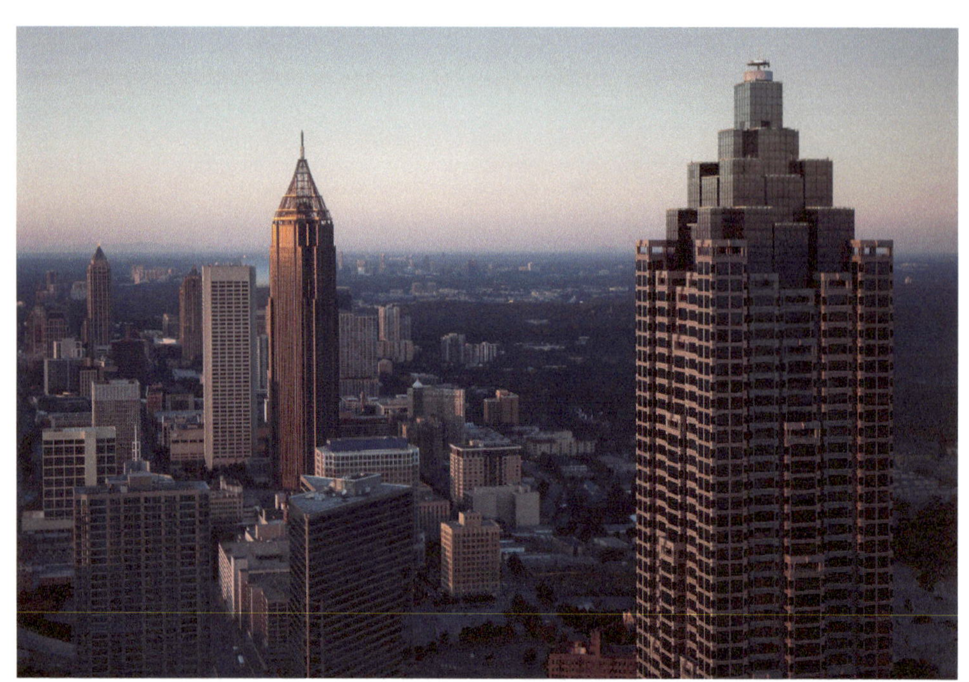
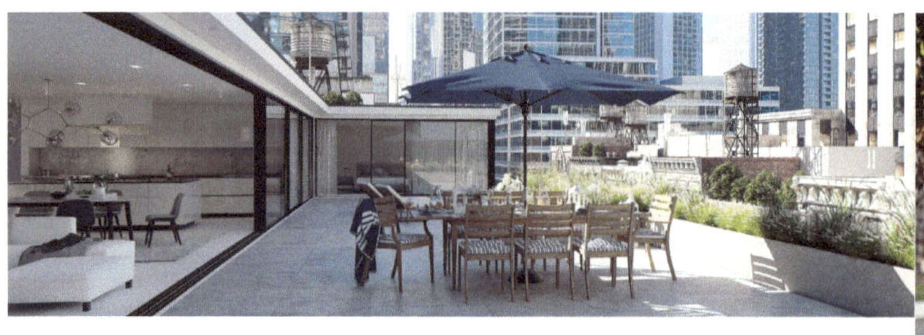
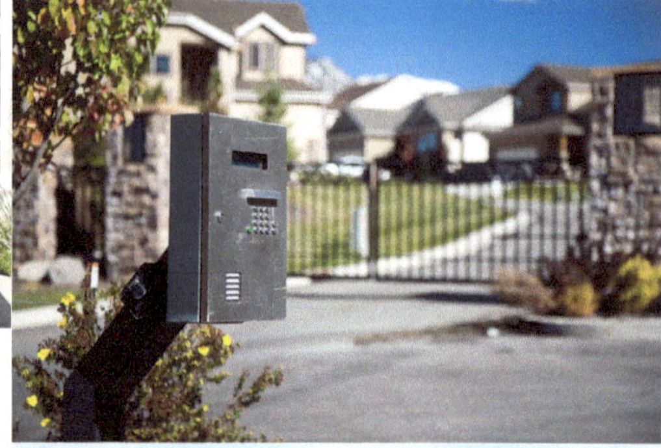
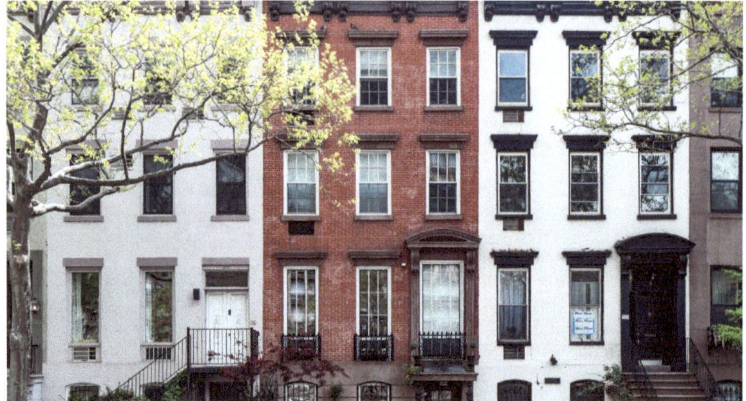
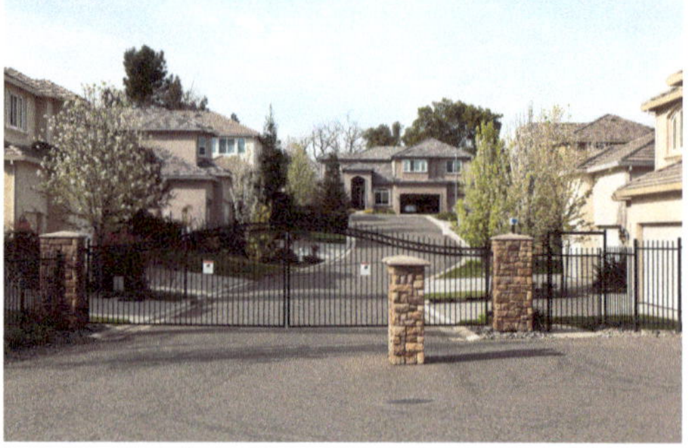
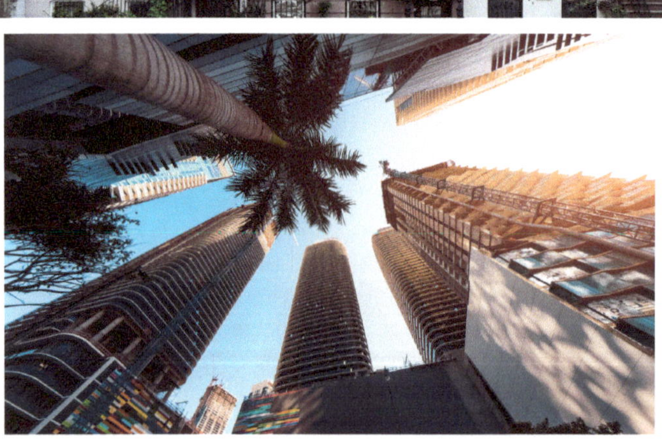
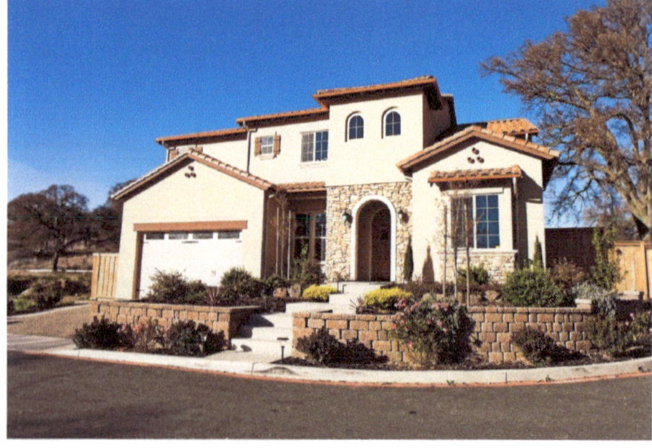

7: New Cars

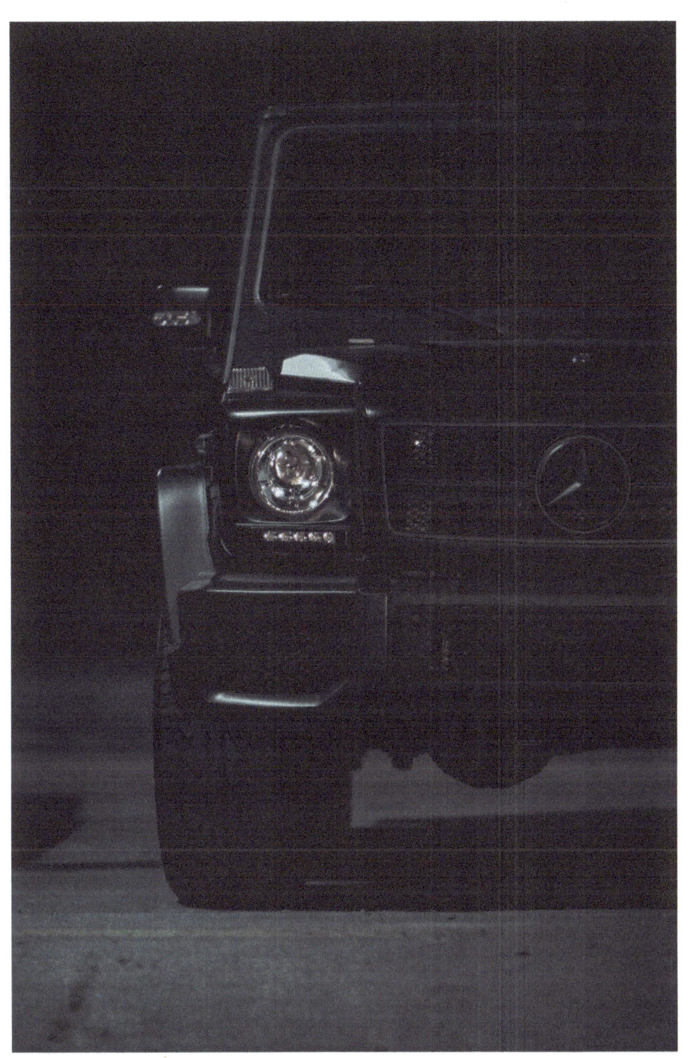

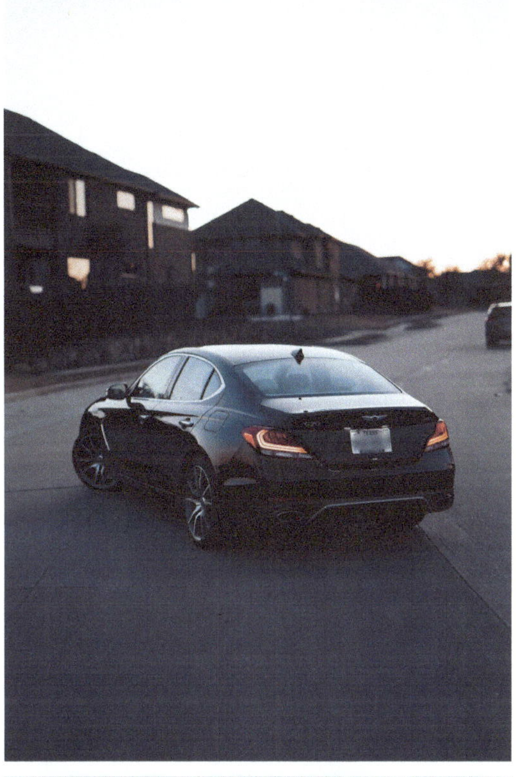

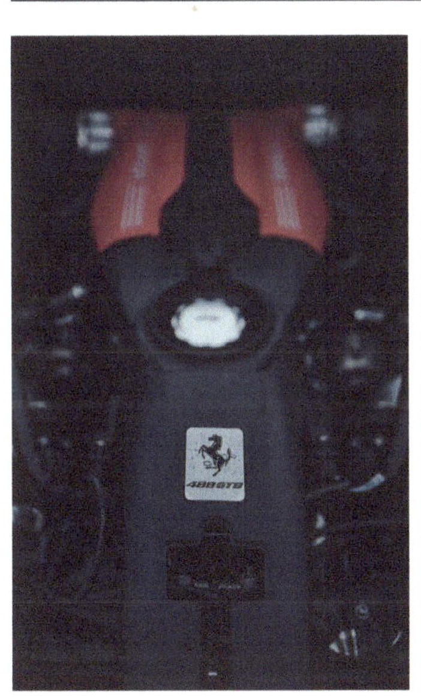

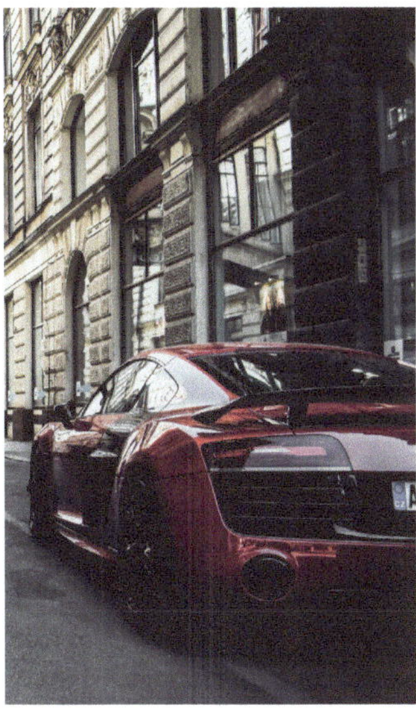

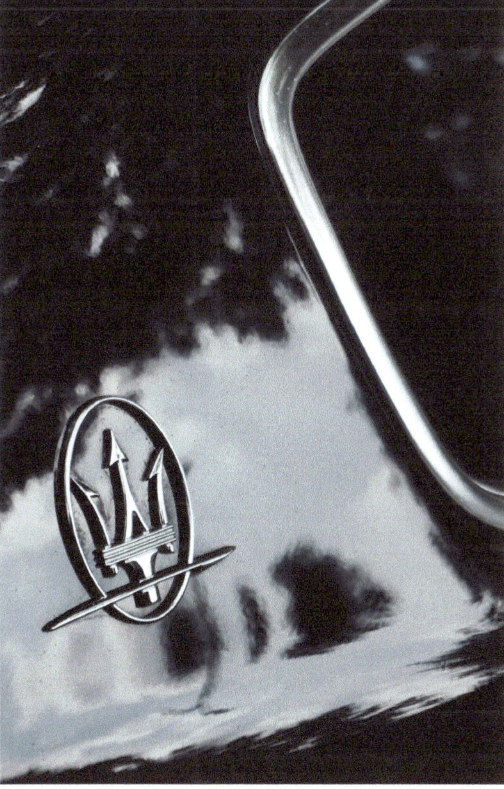

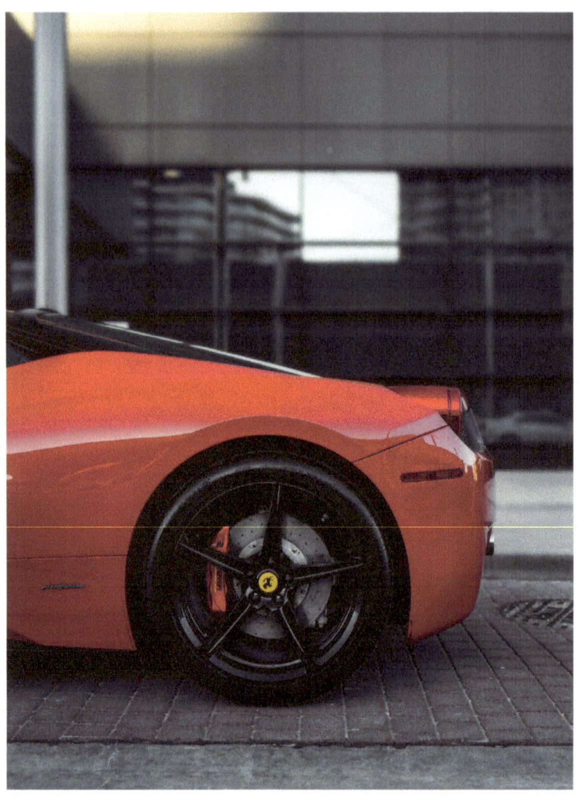
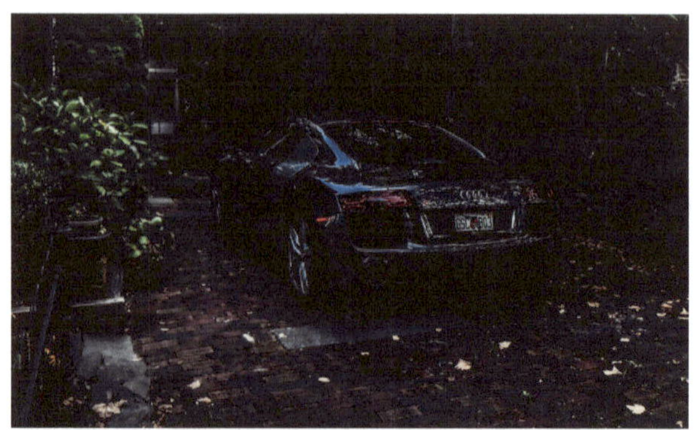
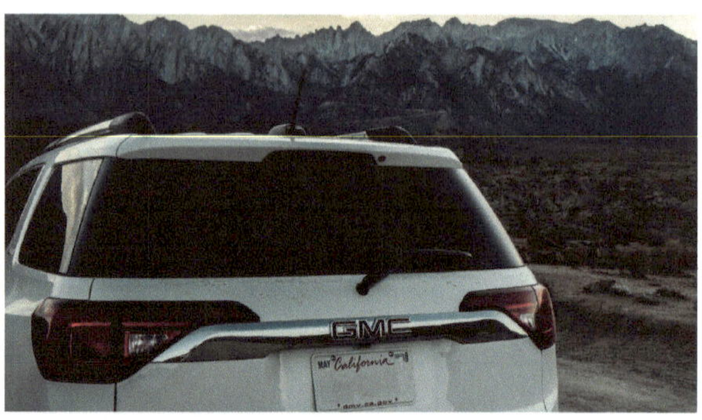
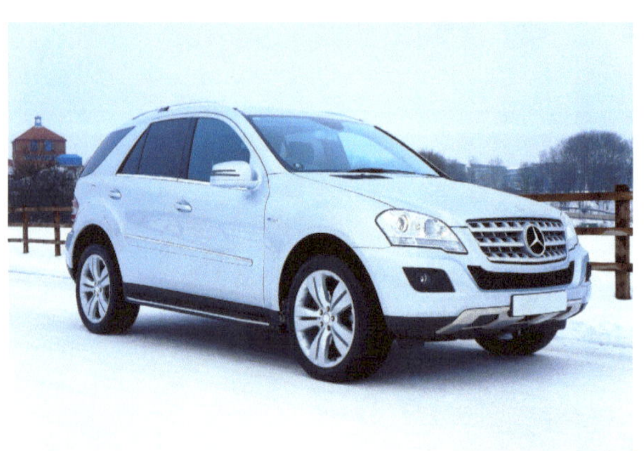
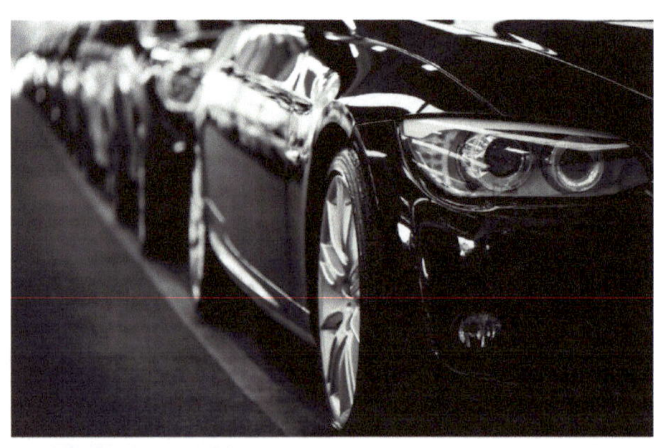
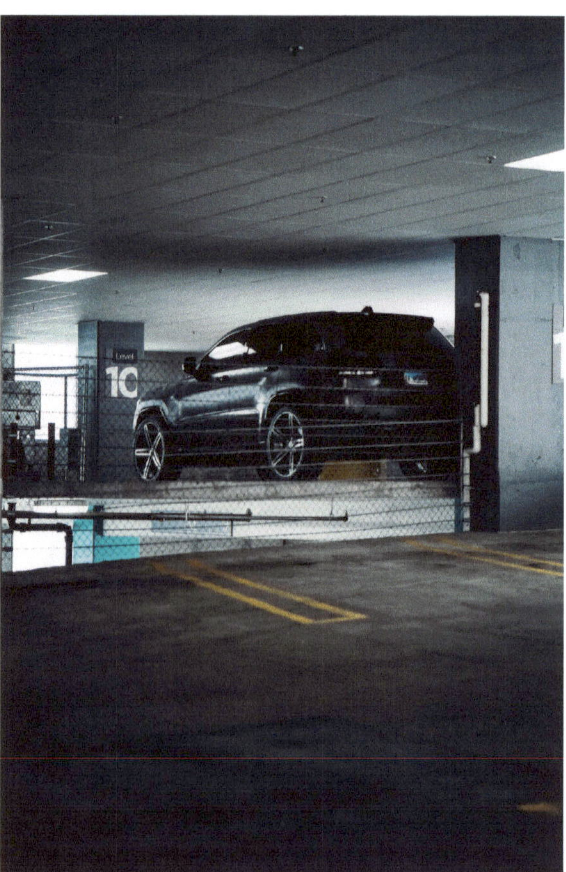

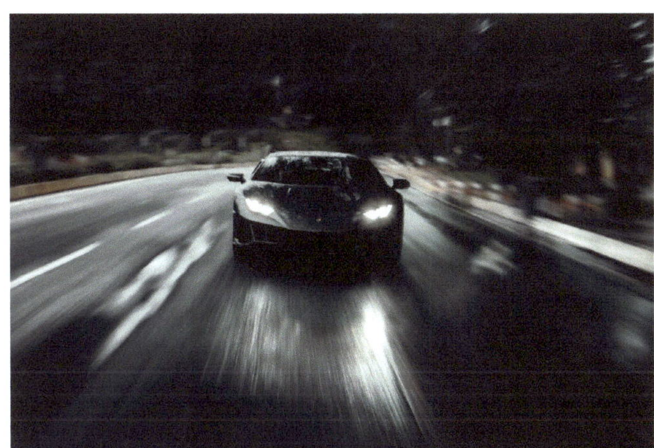
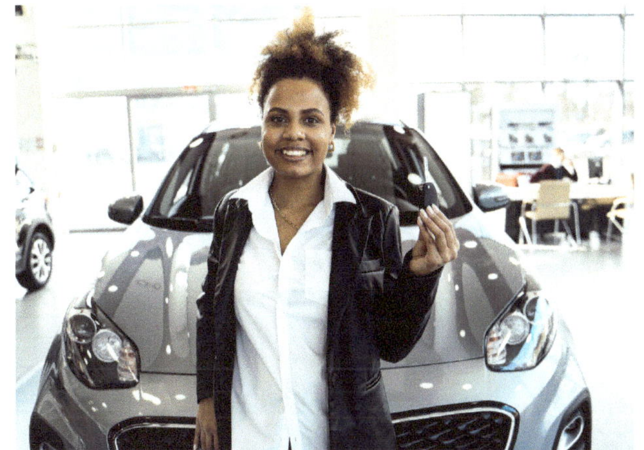
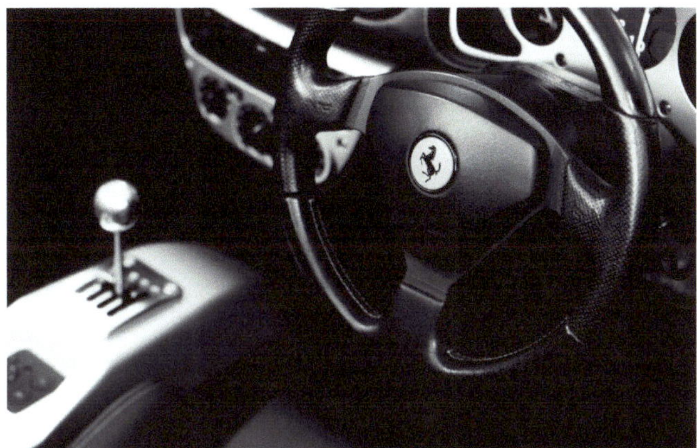
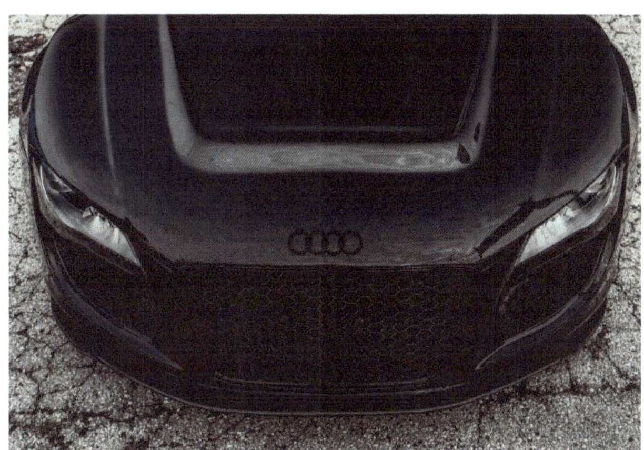
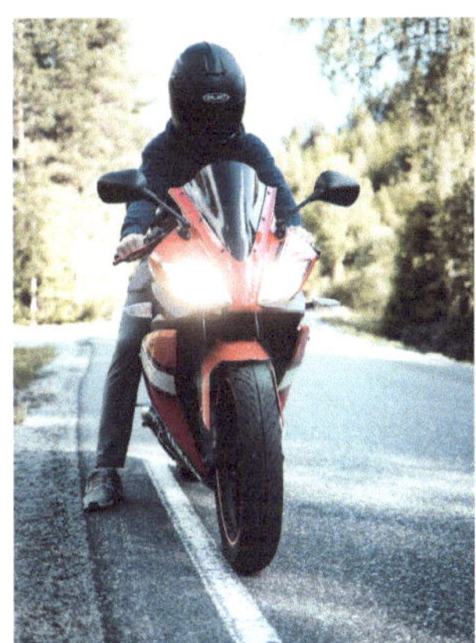
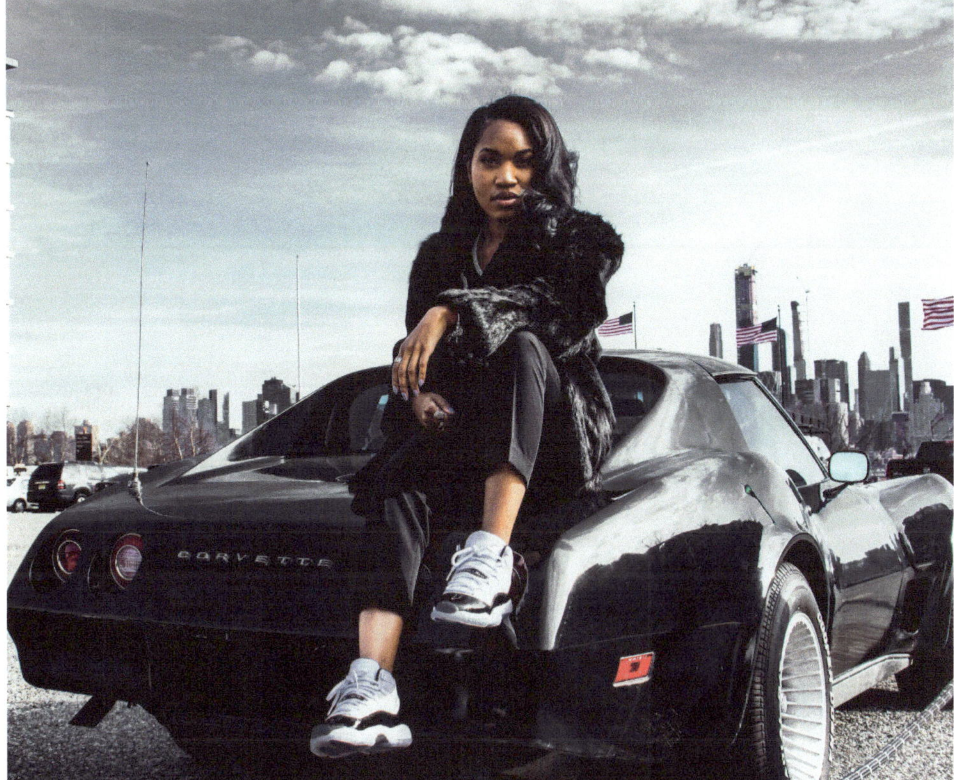
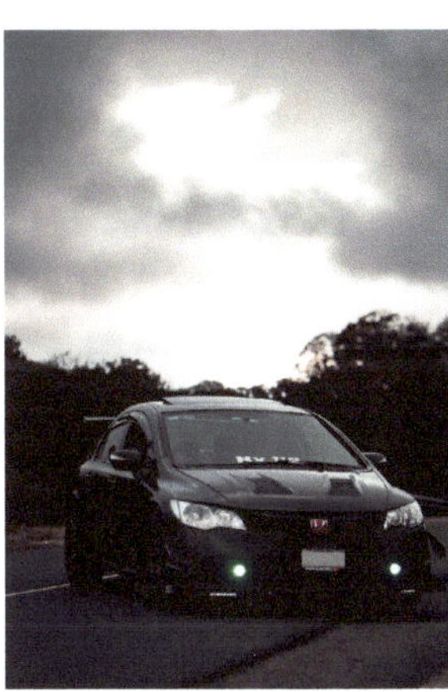

8: Beauty
<u>Because Black is Beautiful</u>

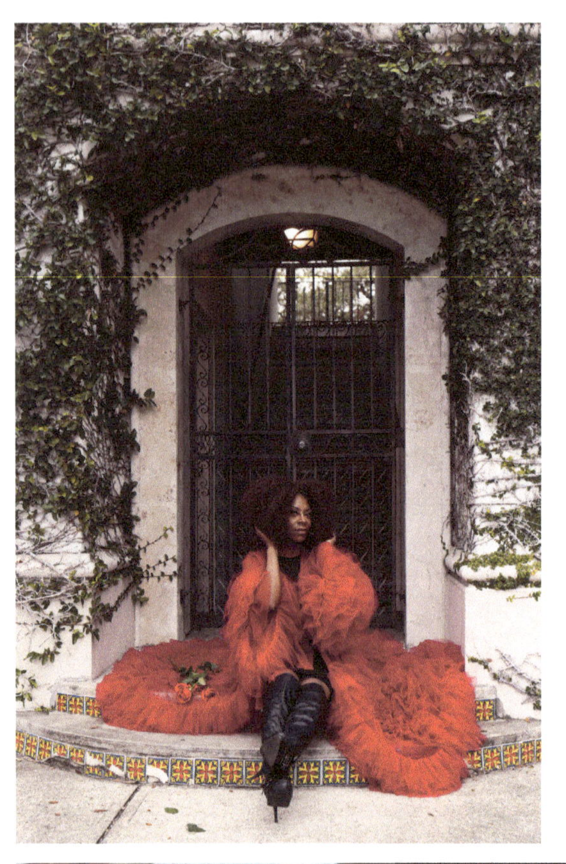

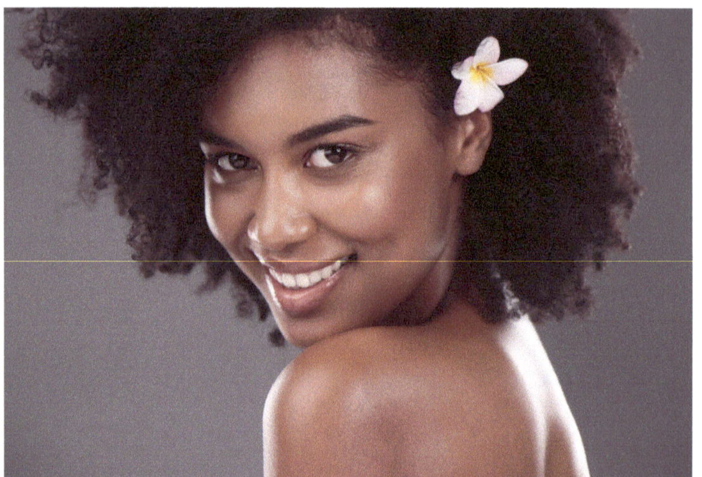

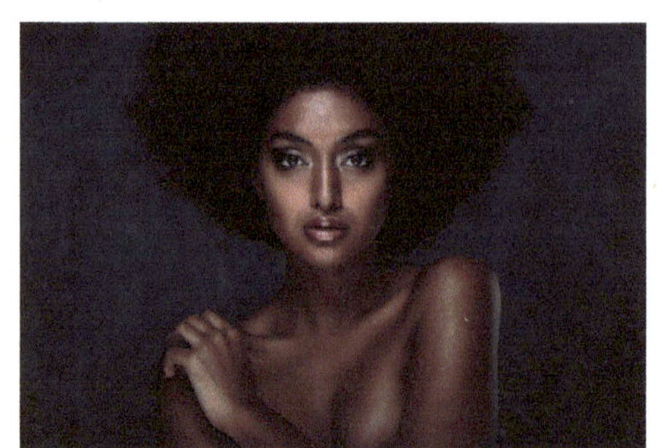

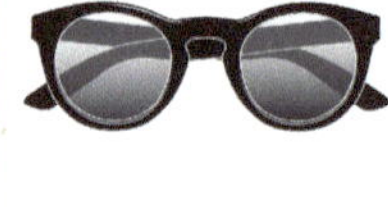

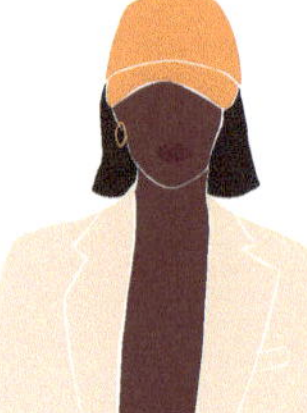

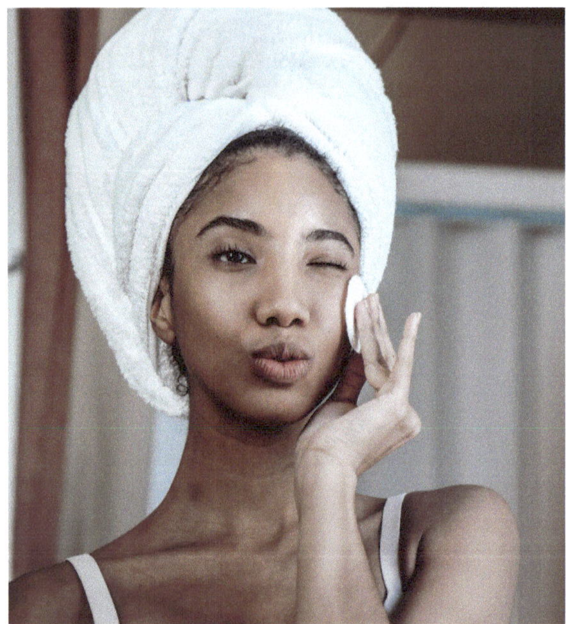

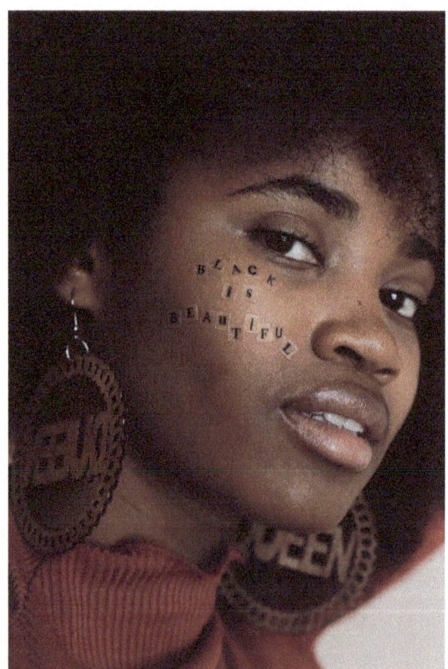

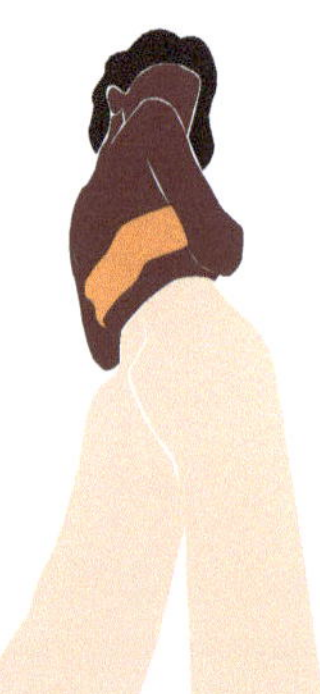

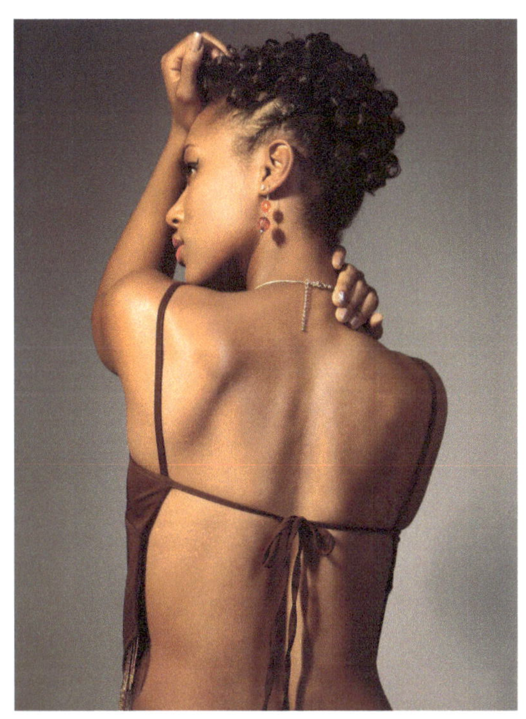
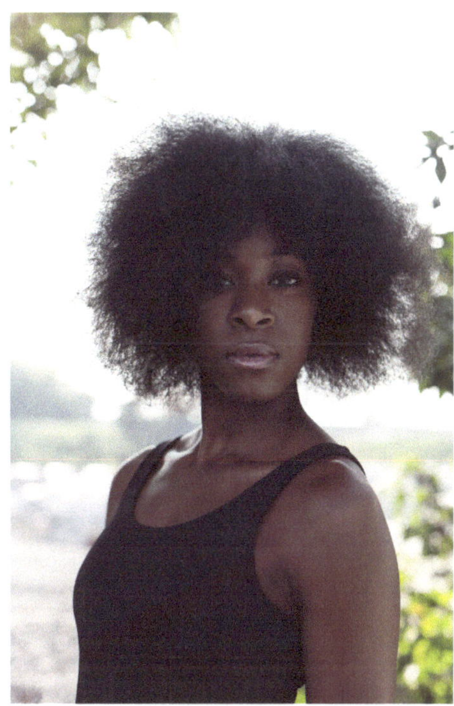
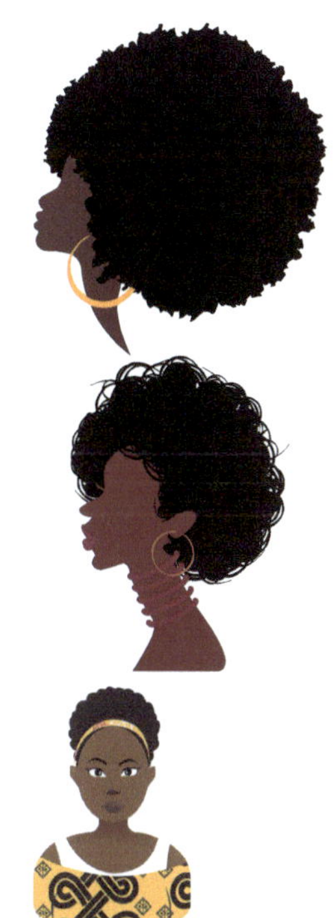
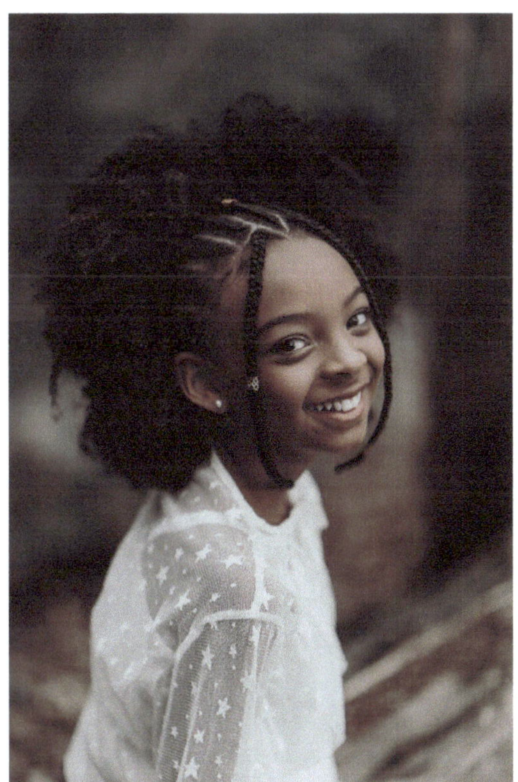
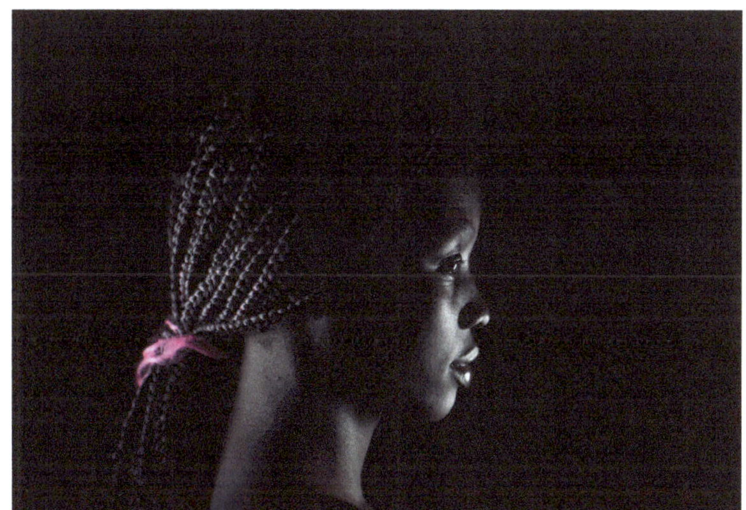
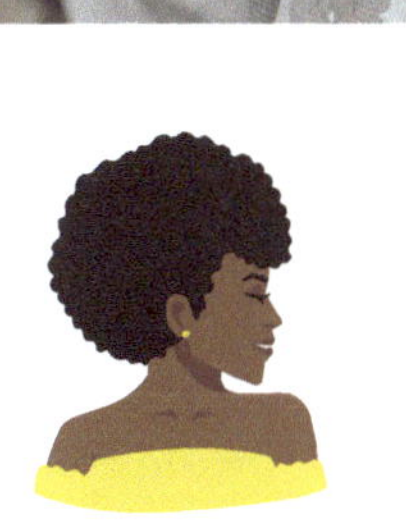
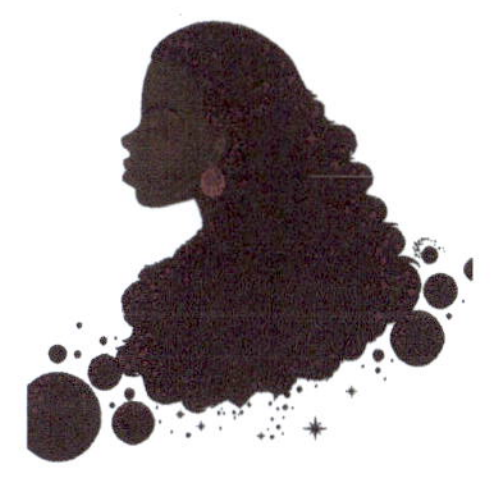
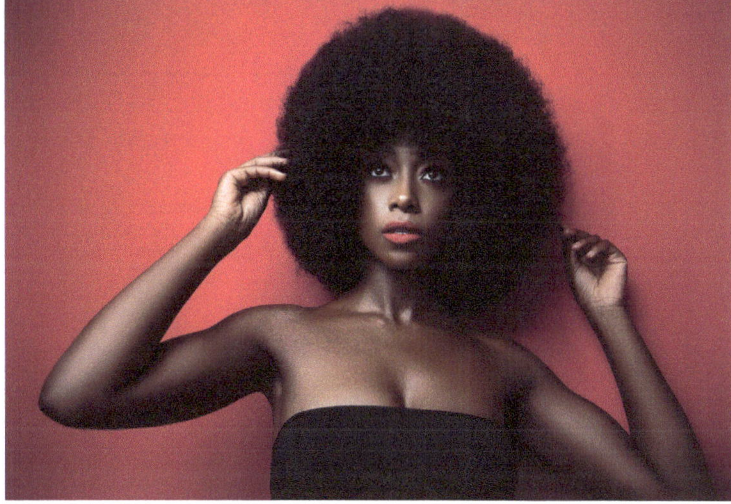

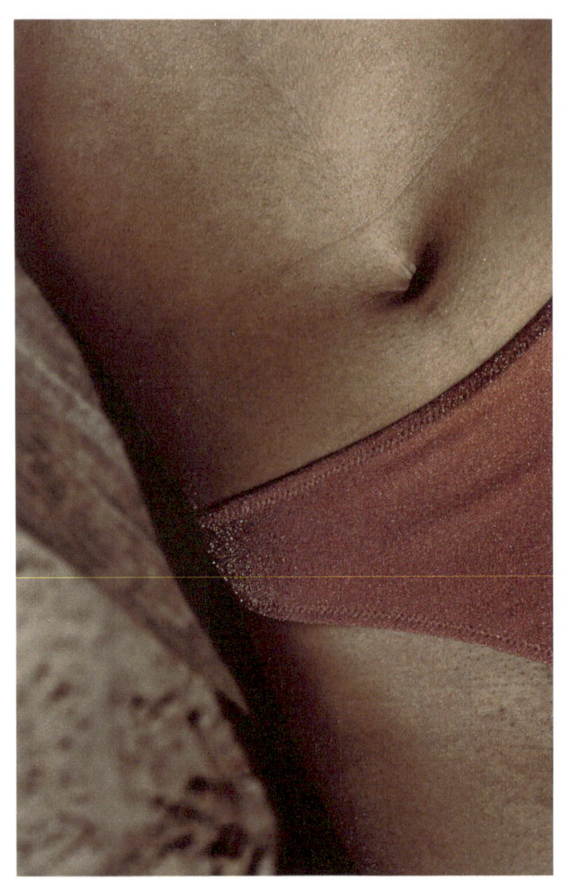
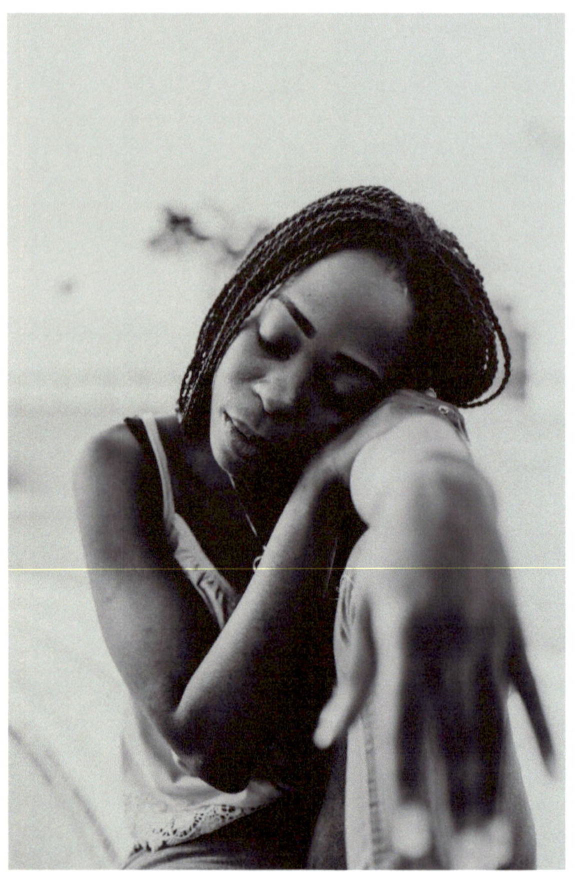
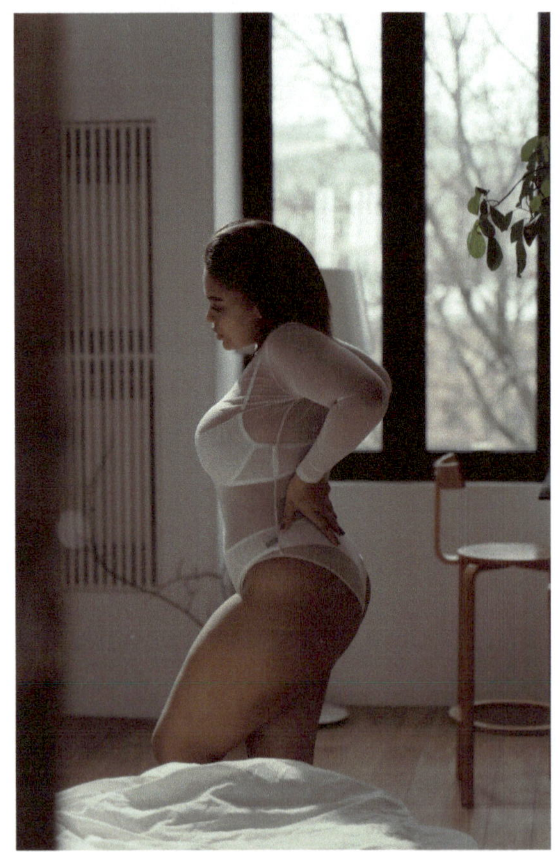
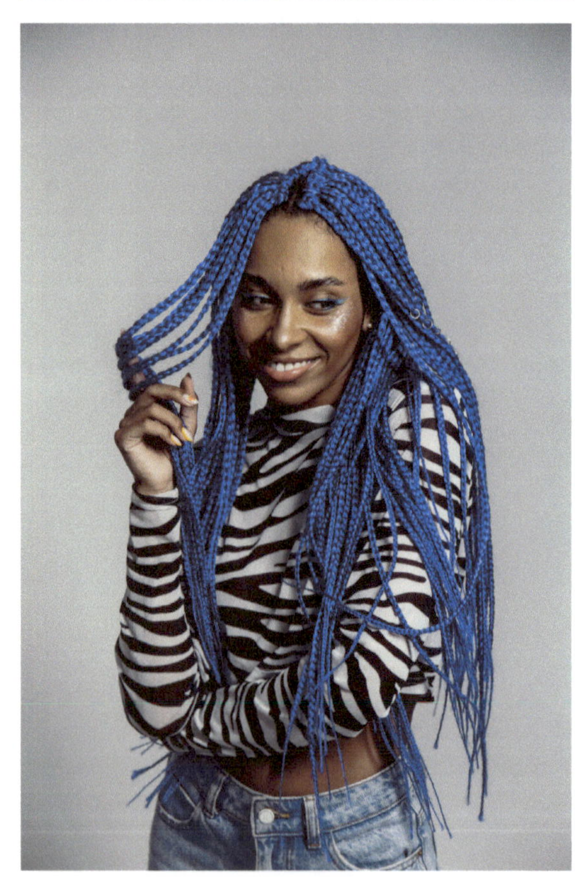

9: Fun, Hobbies & Sports

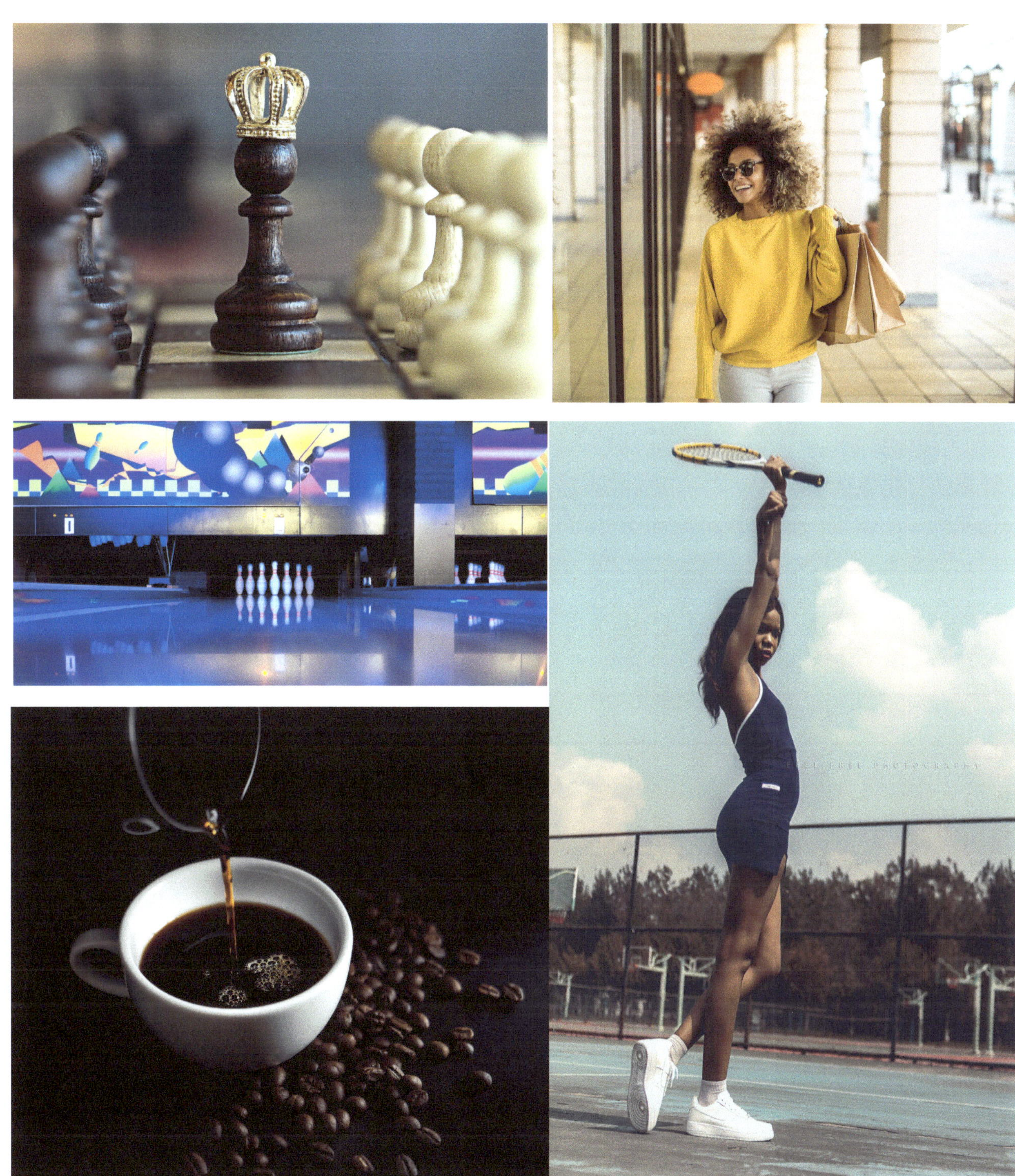

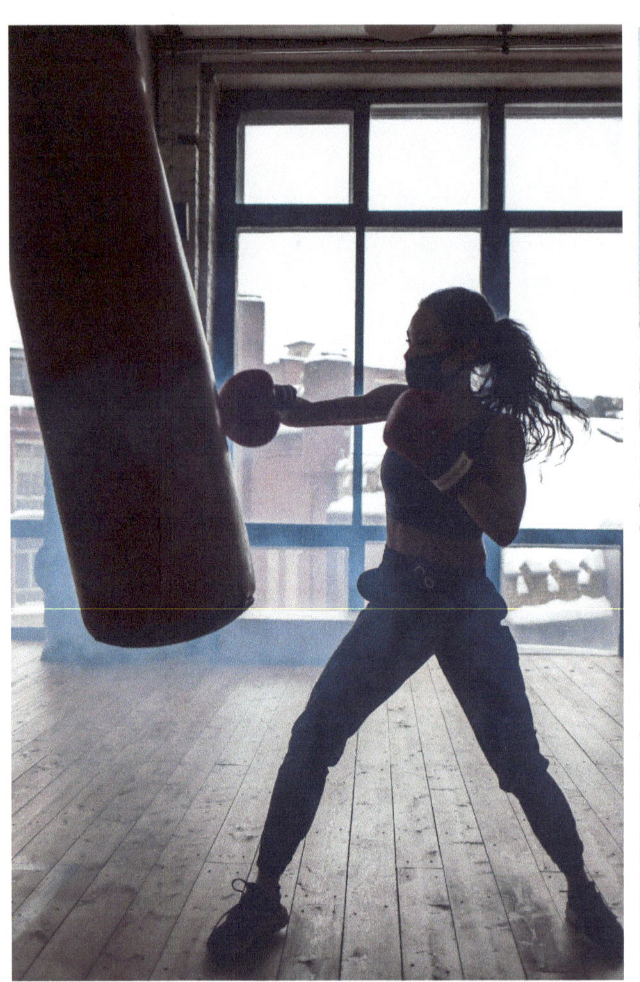
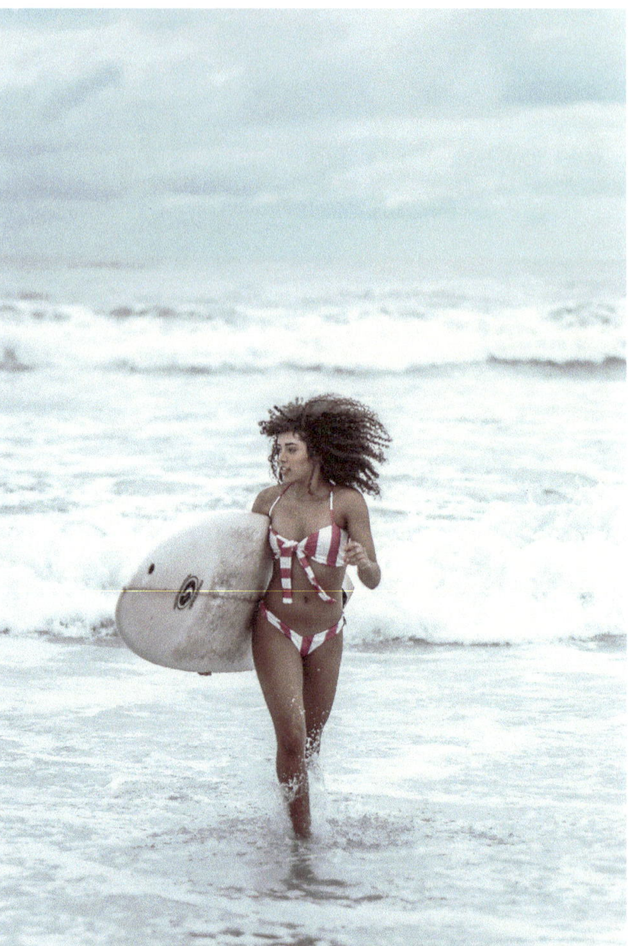
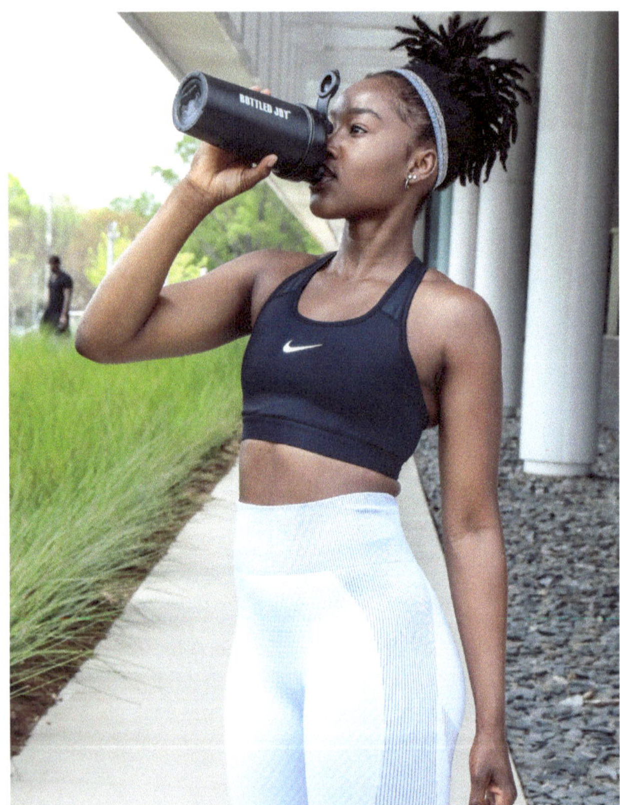
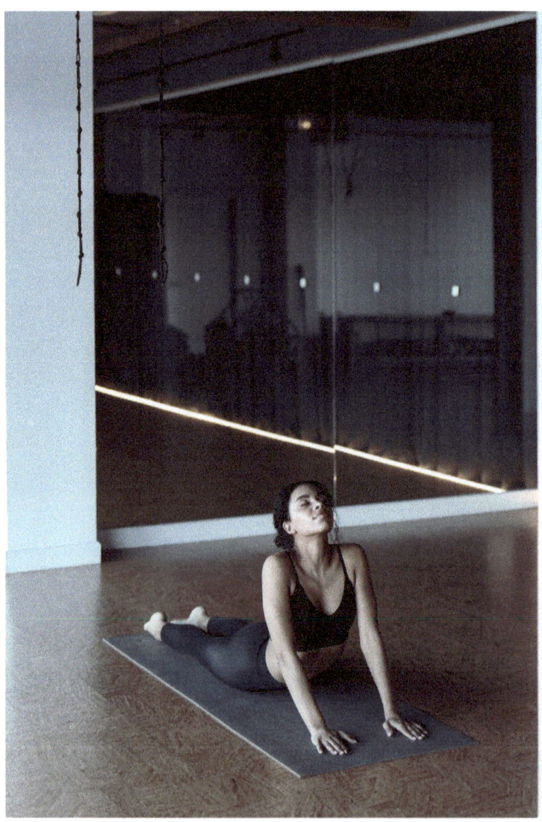

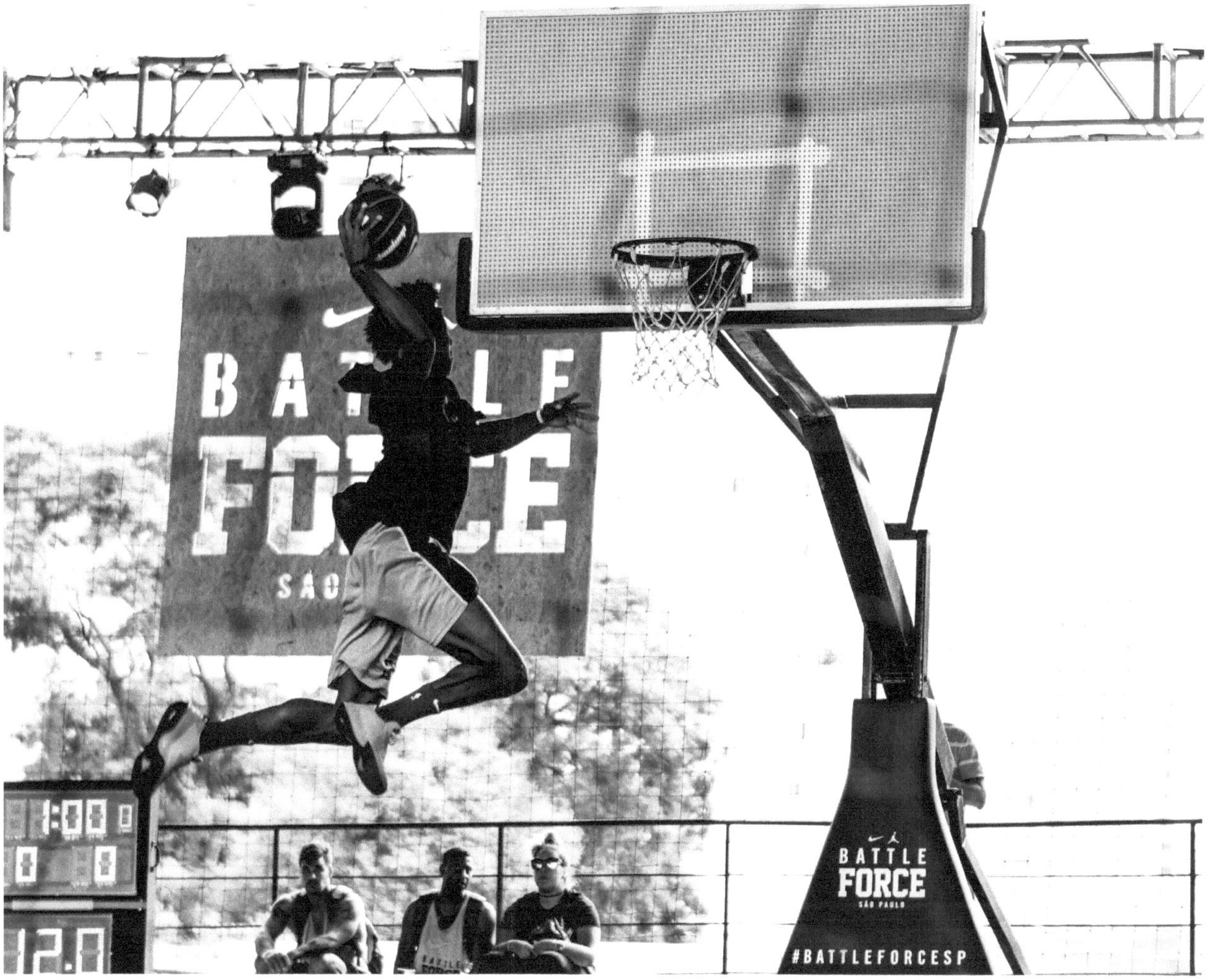

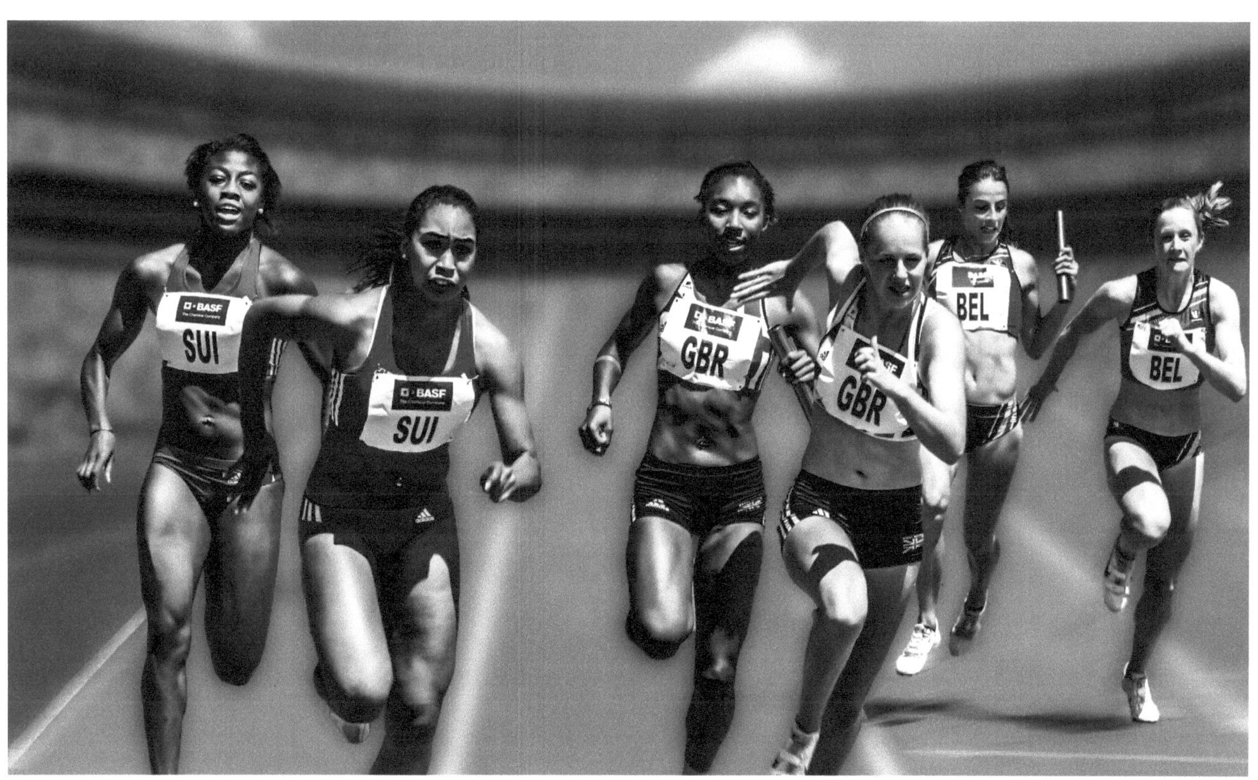

10: Body Positivity & Health

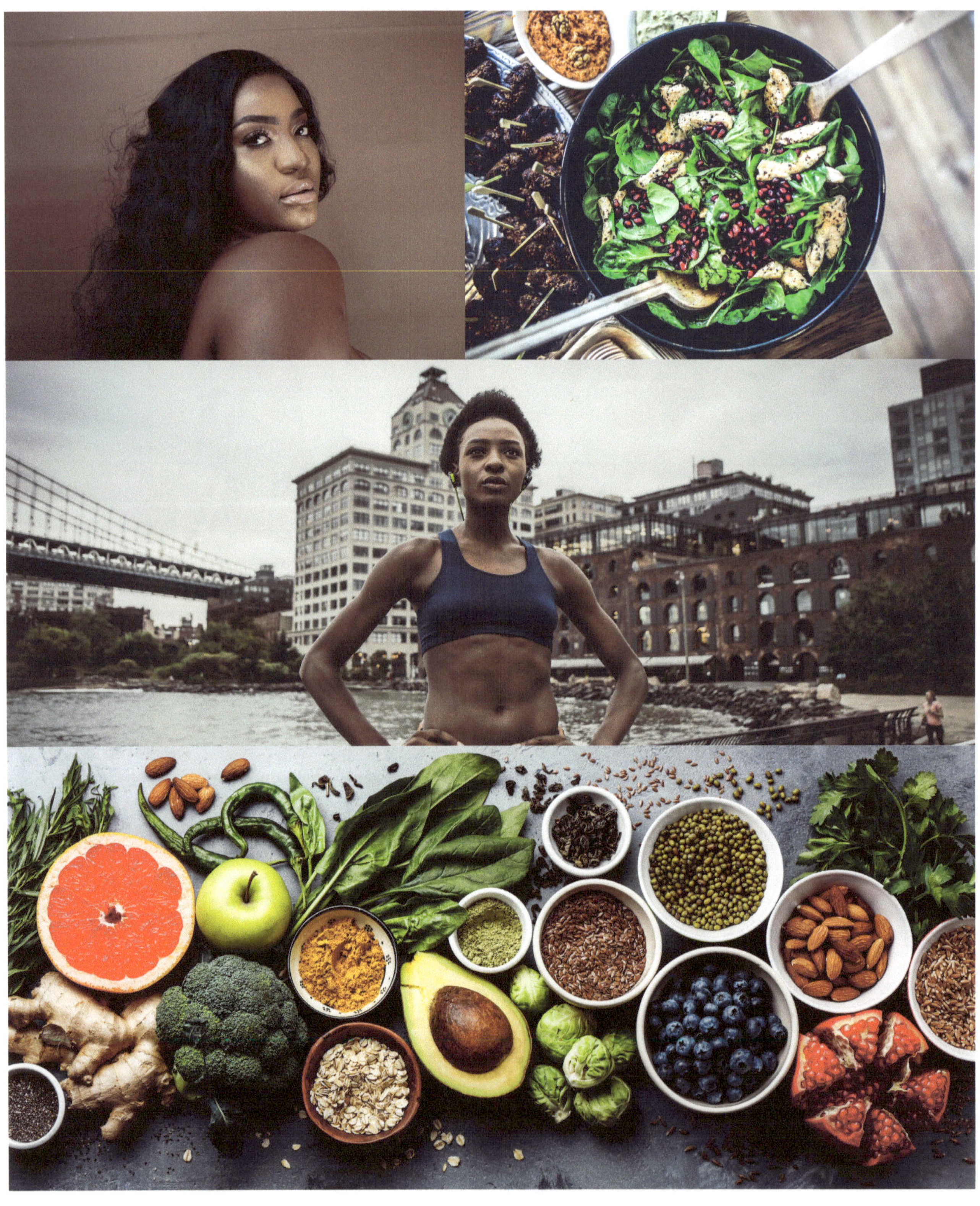

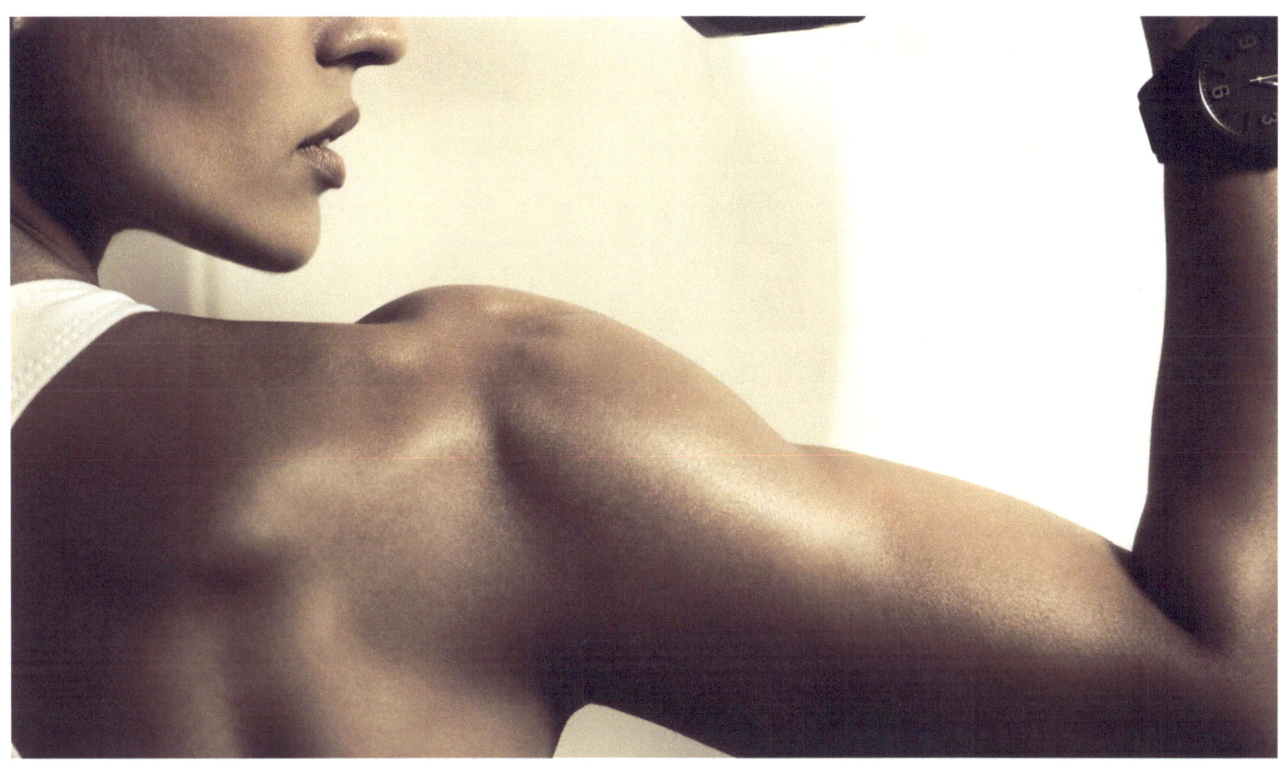

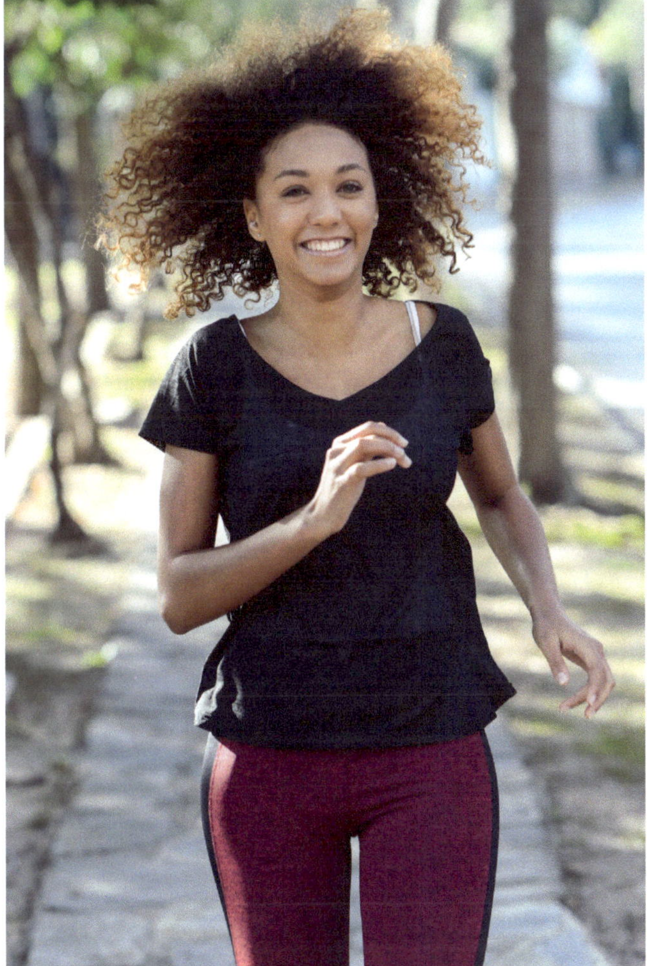

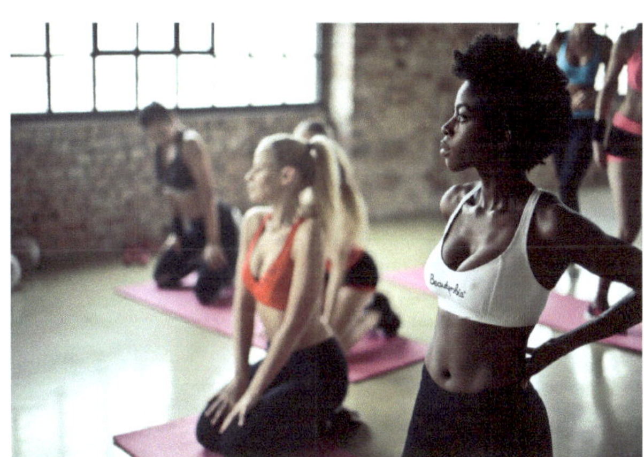

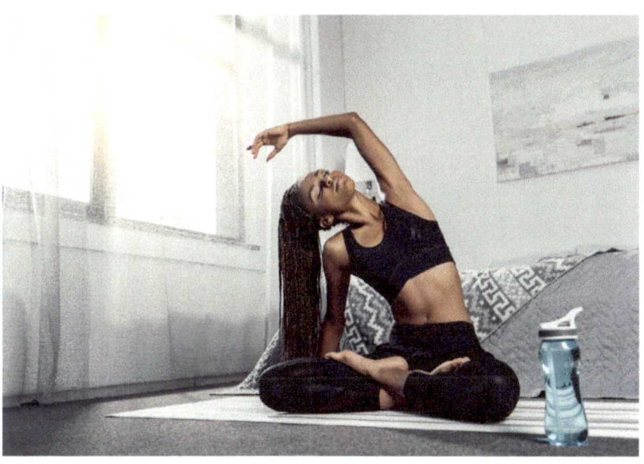

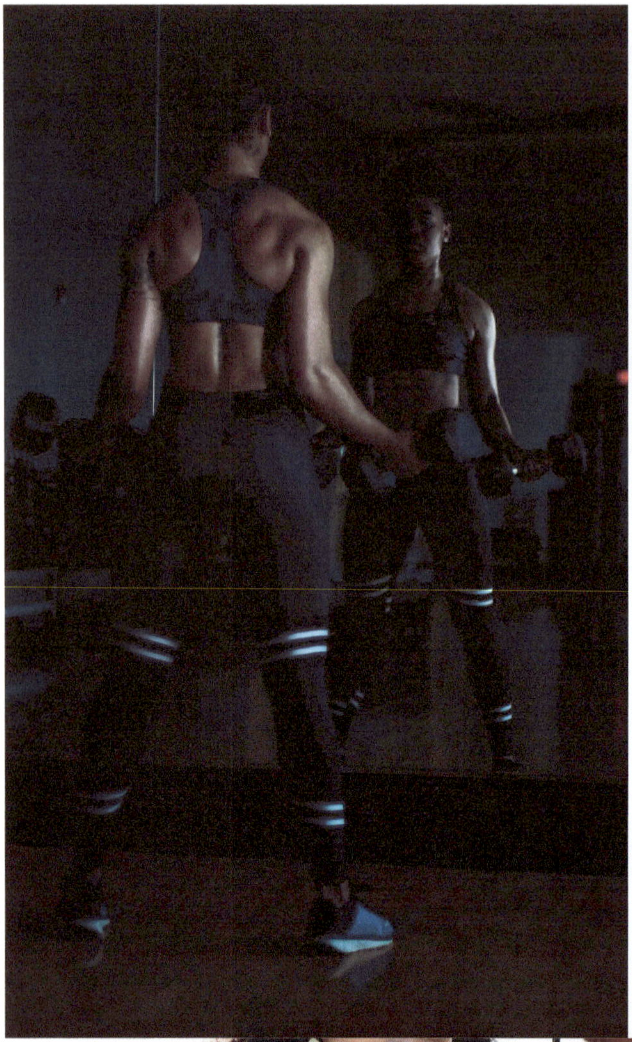

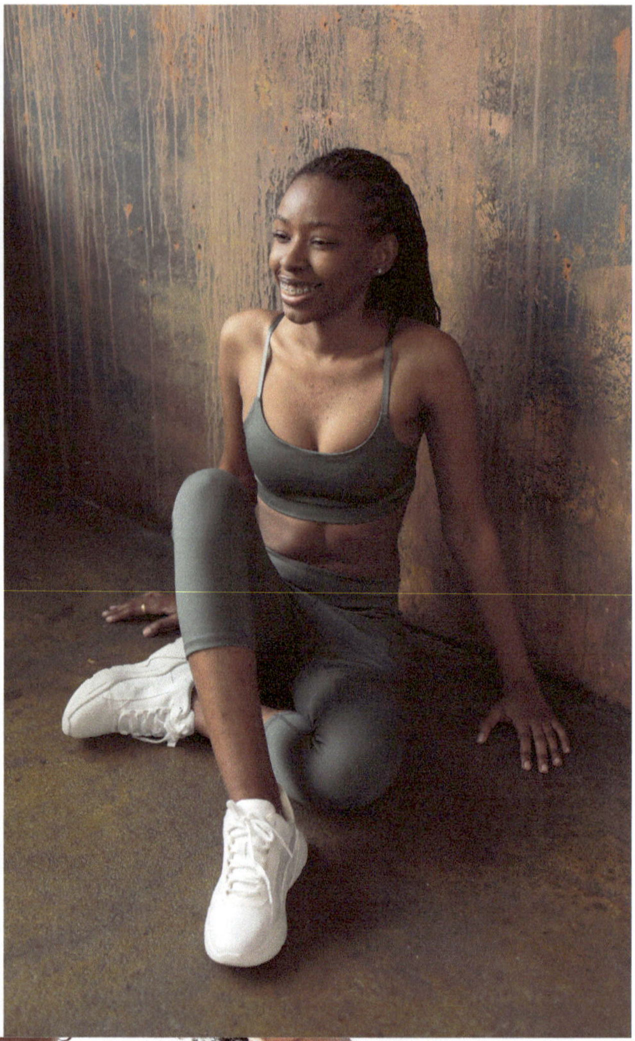

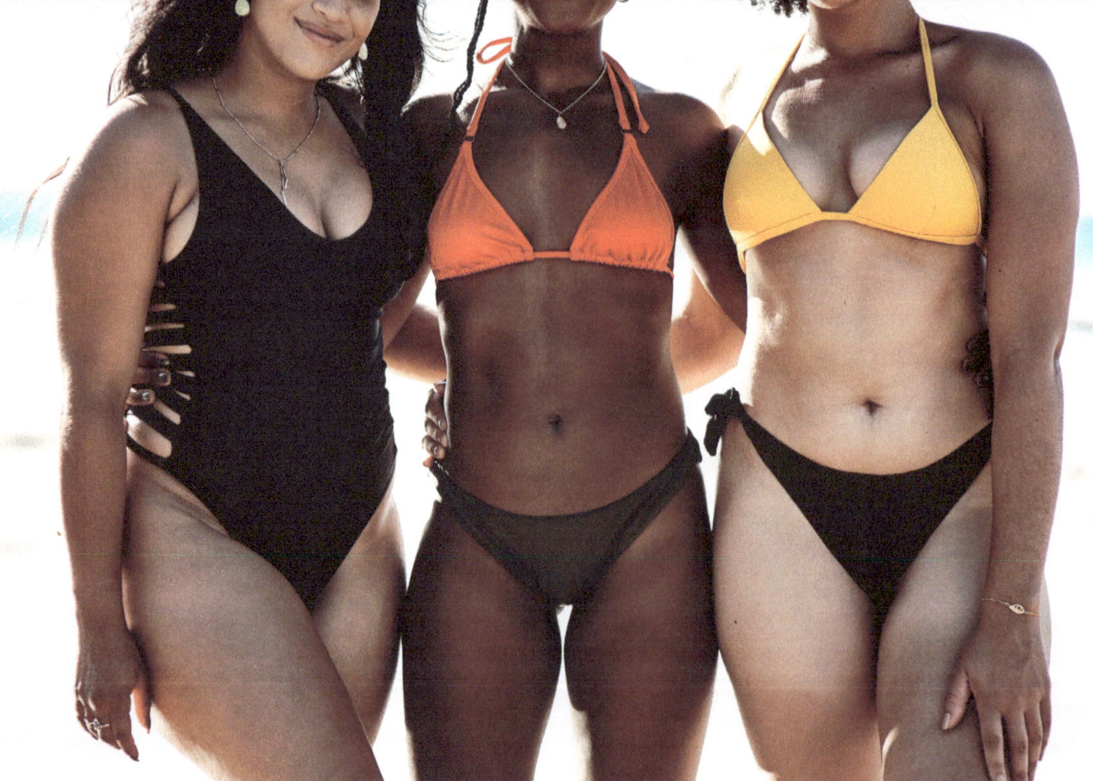

11: Vacations & Travel

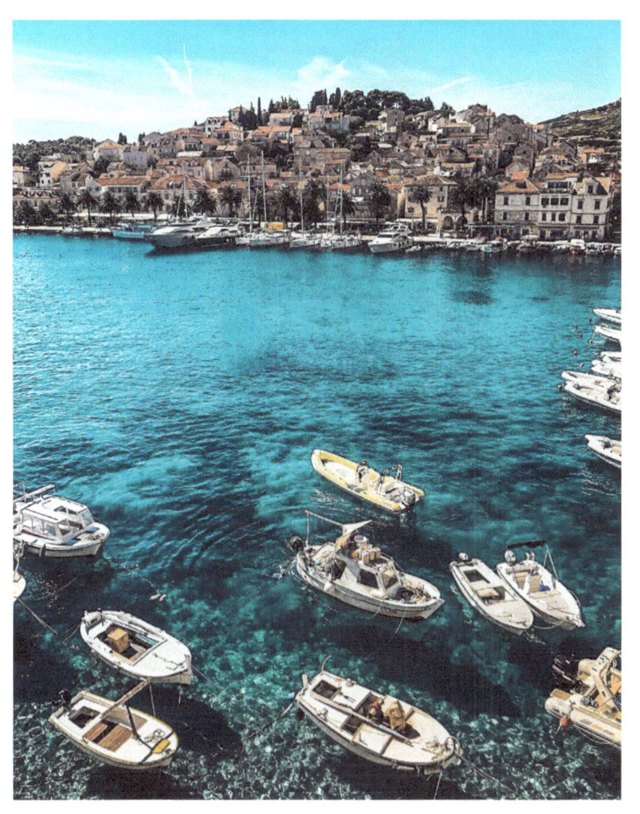
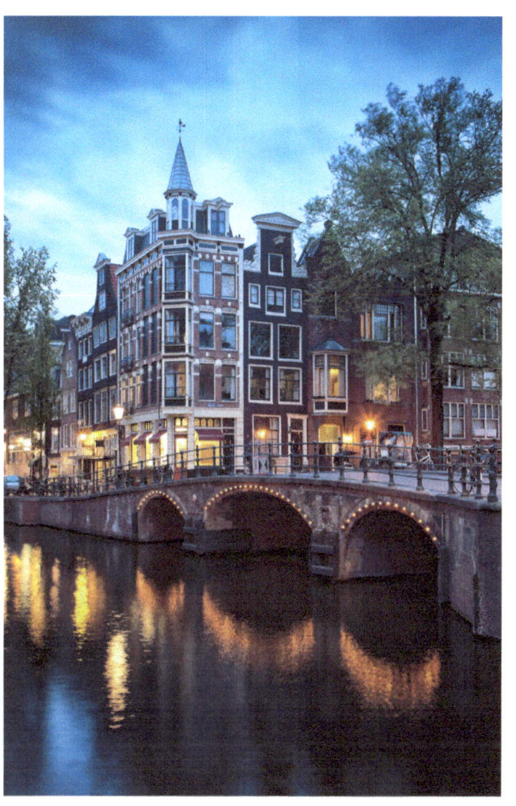
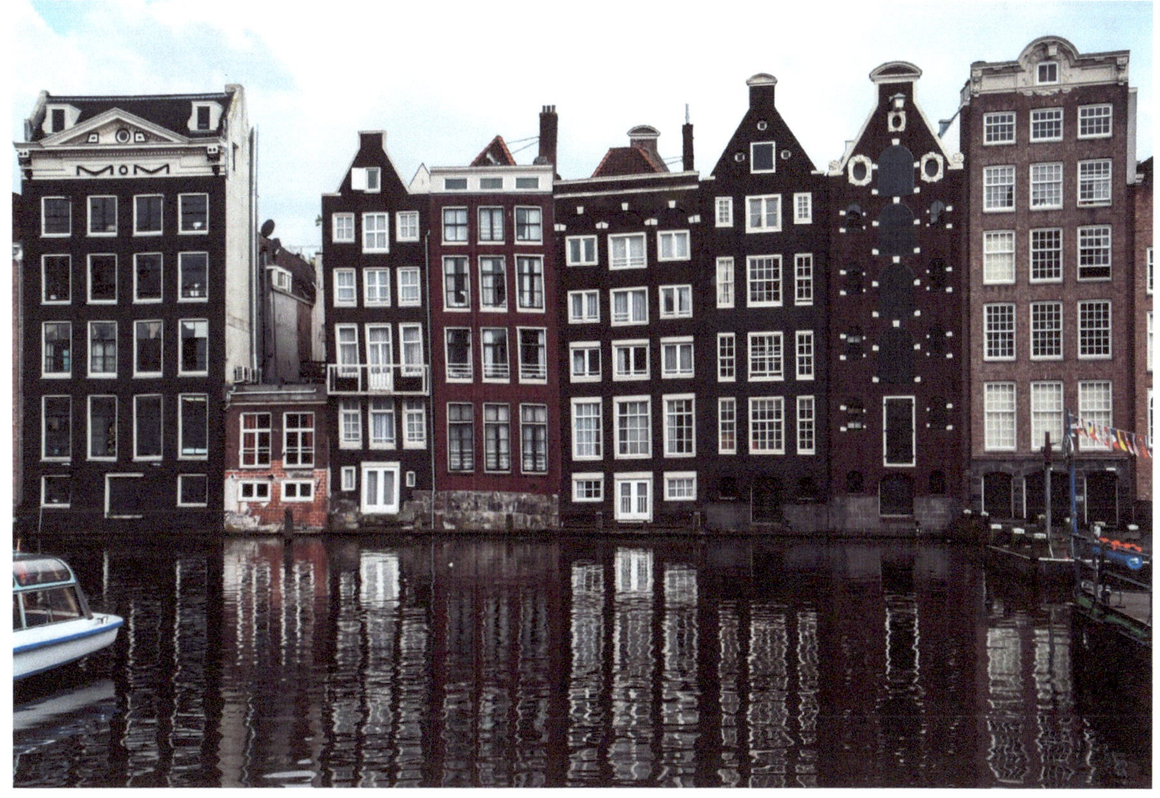

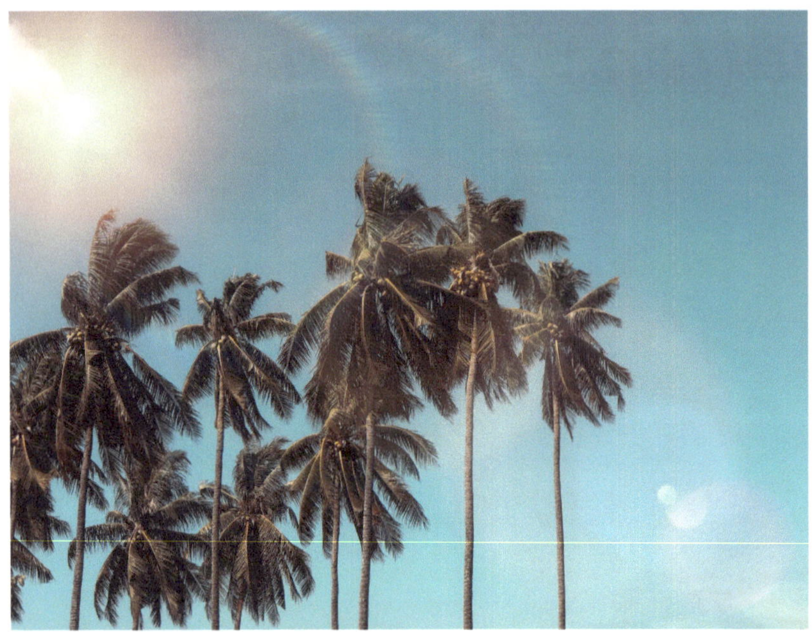

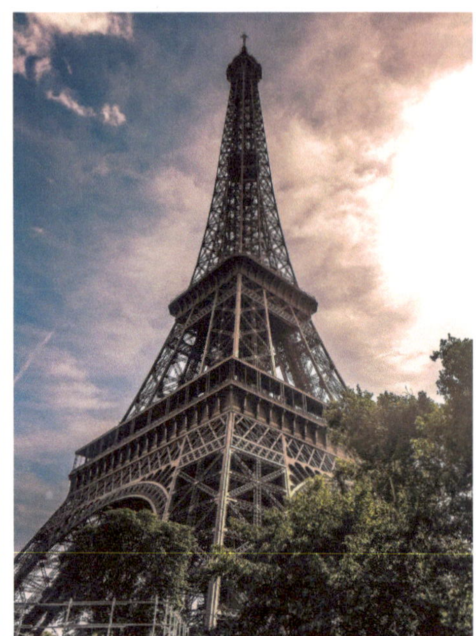

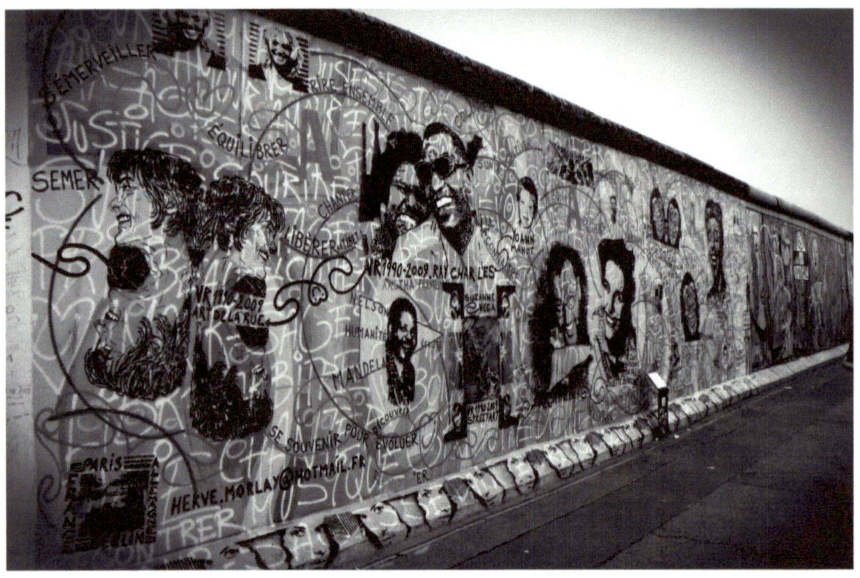

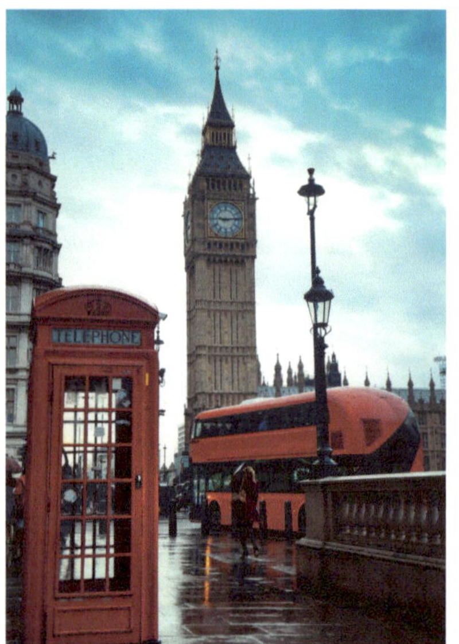

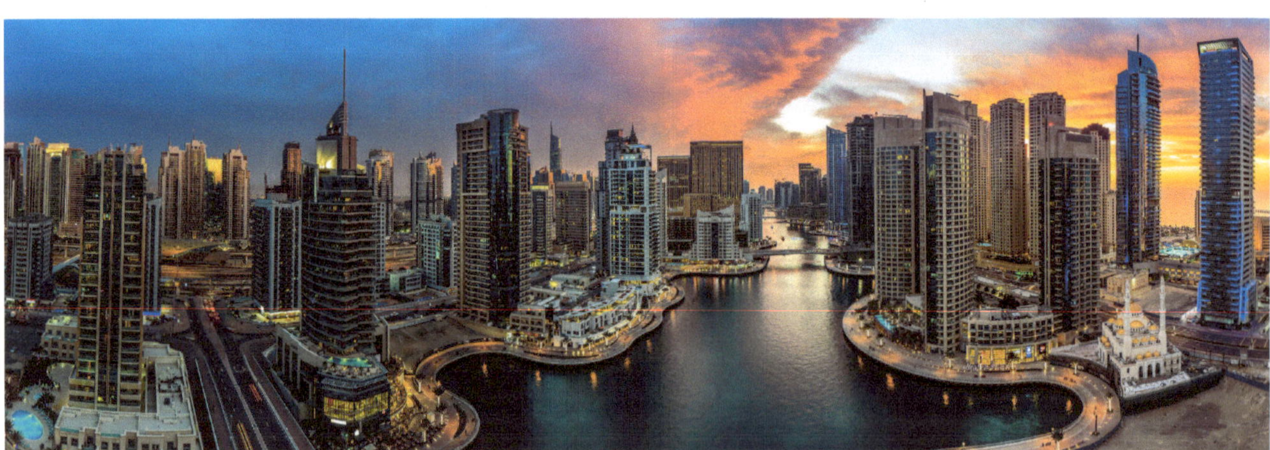

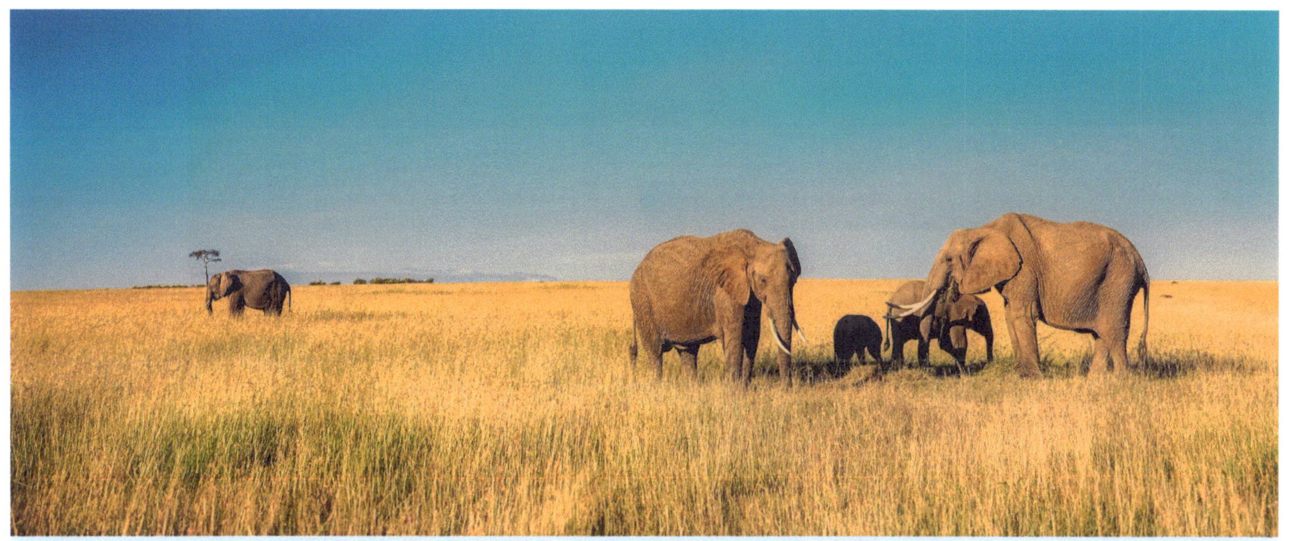

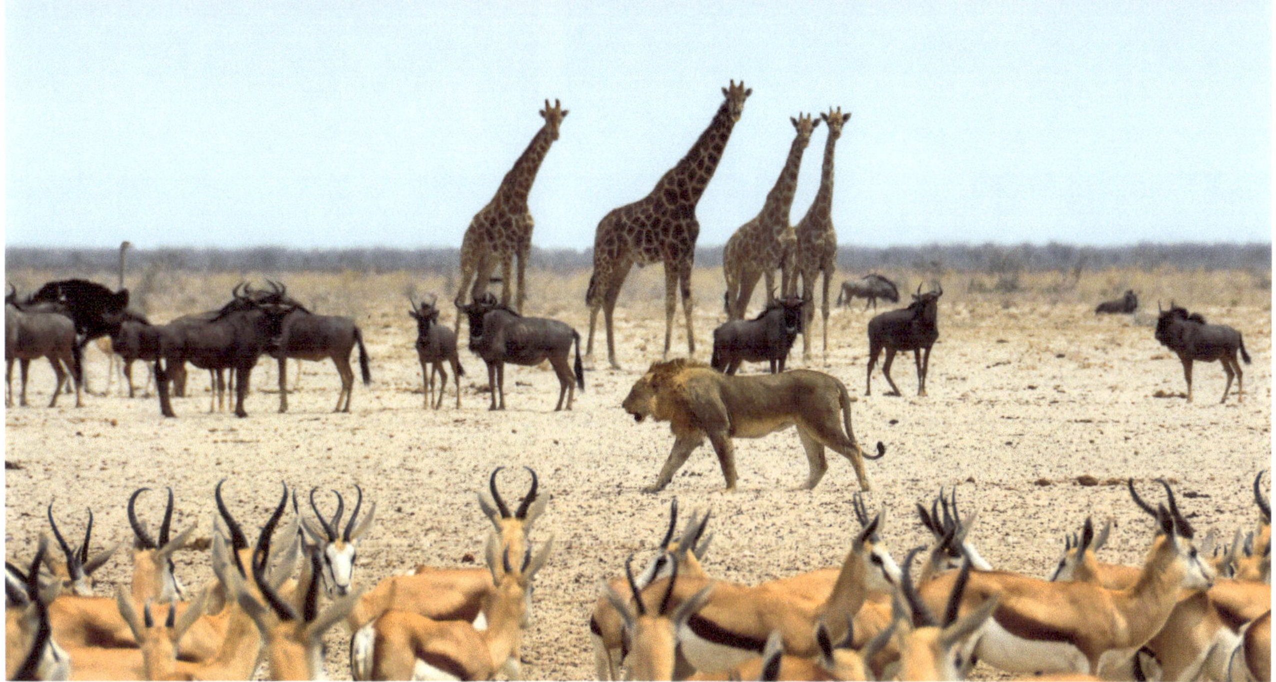

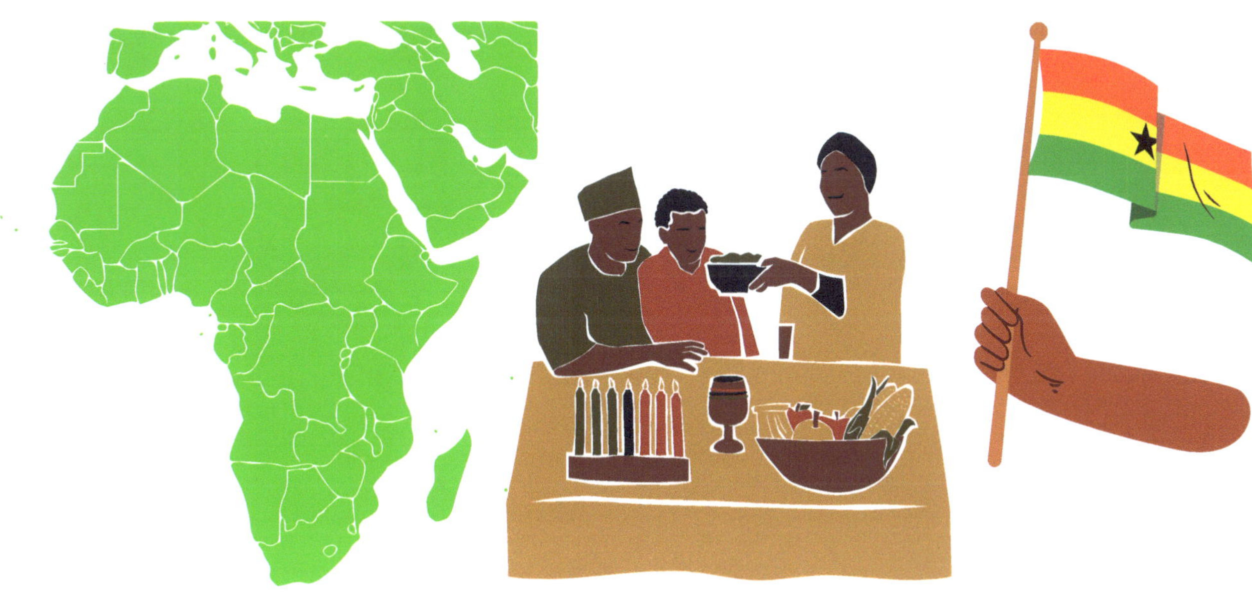

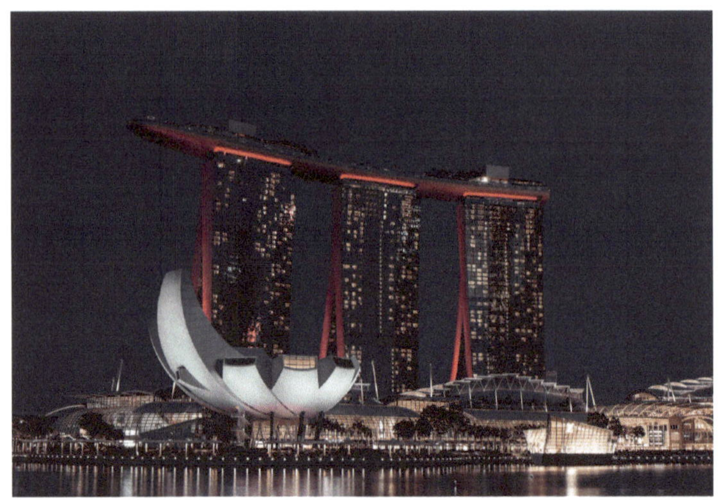
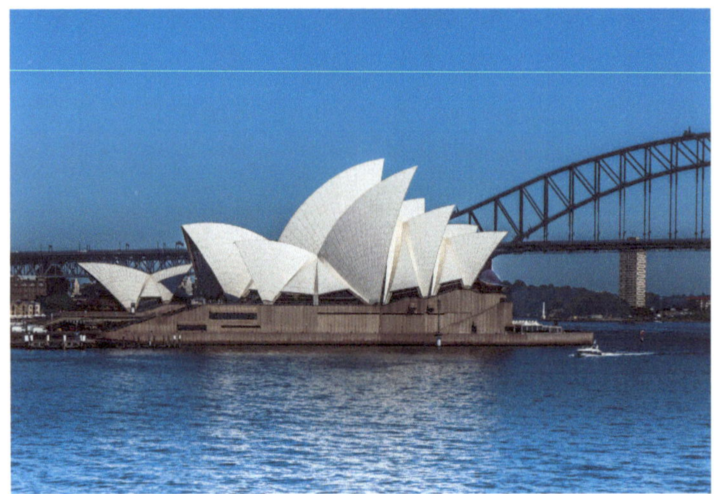
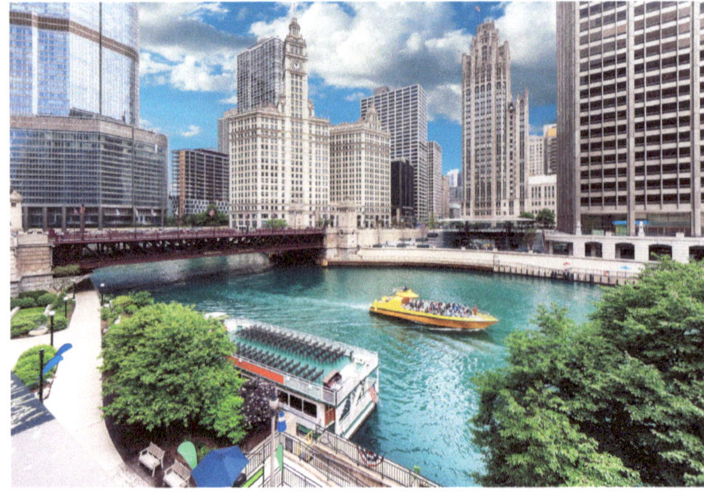
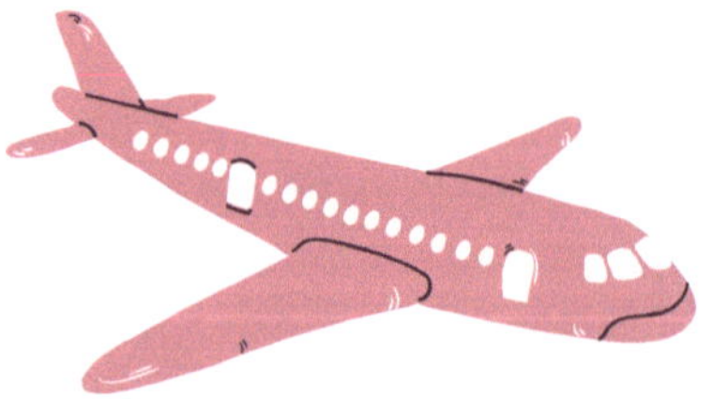
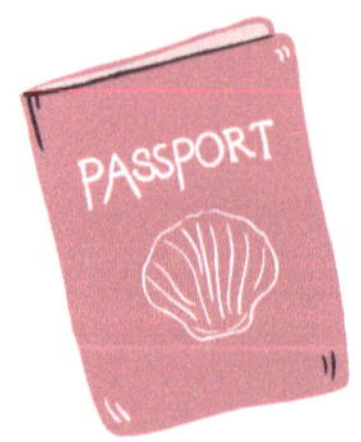
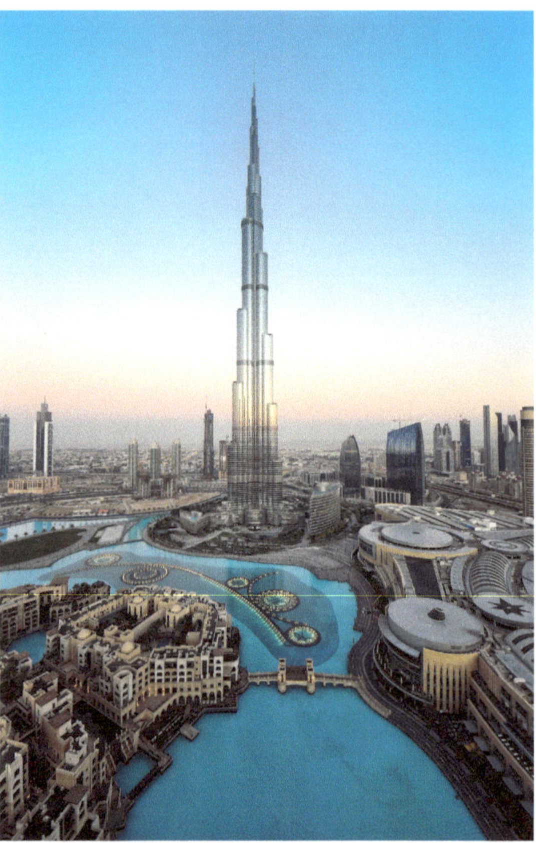
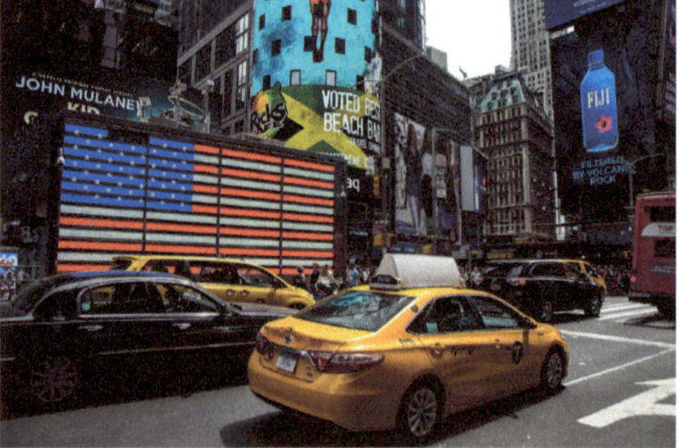

JOHN MULANE
VOTED BE
BEACH B
FIJI

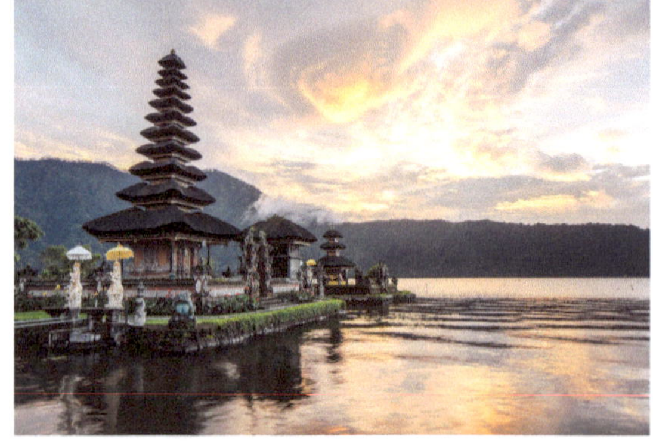

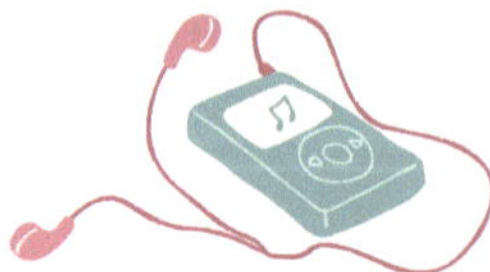

We hope you enjoyed the photos, graphics & clipart from this book - if you did, please leave us a 5* review on Amazon - It really helps our new publishing company, more than you could imagine!

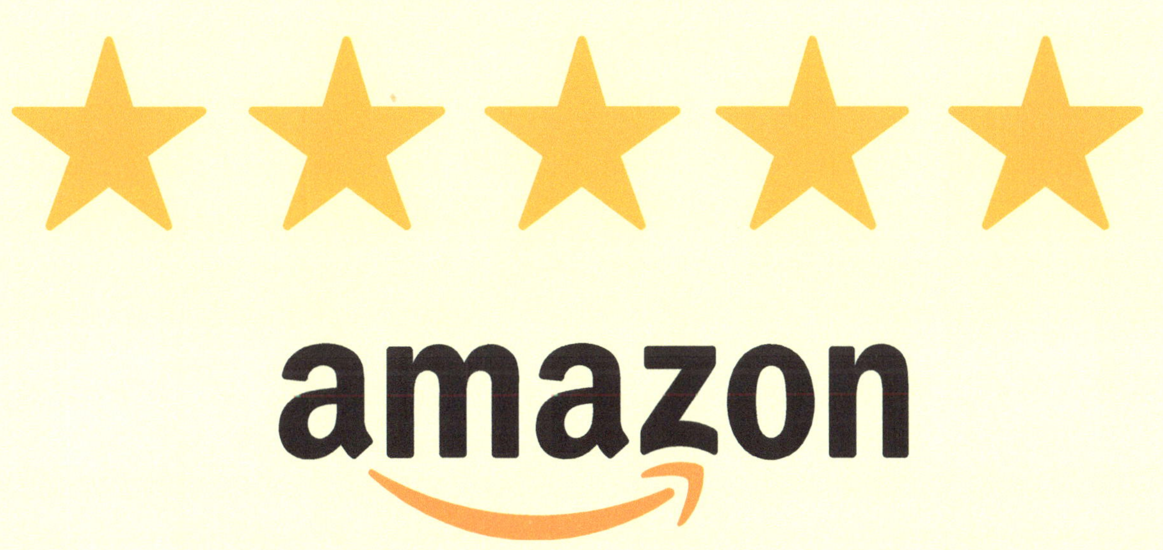

We pray that they will help you to manifest your ideal life. After all, happiness comes from progress - so if you can make steps to get closer to your goals, you will be happy.

Check out our in-depth guide to Financial Freedom for Black Women - we expect it will be published by the beginning of April!

coming soon!

Search "Tamika Gilzene" on Amazon to find it!